THE CANONS OF THE
CHURCH OF ENGLAND

THE CANONS OF
THE CHURCH OF ENGLAND

Canons Ecclesiastical
promulged by the Convocations of
Canterbury and York in
1964 and 1969

LONDON S·P·C·K 1969

First published in 1969
by S.P.C.K.
Holy Trinity Church
Marylebone Road
London N.W. 1

Printed in Great Britain
at the University Printing House, Cambridge

SBN 281 02329 8 (paper)
281 02330 1 (cased)

CONTENTS

INTRODUCTION

by the Archbishops of Canterbury and York

The publication of the present volume marks the completion of the main work of Canon Law revision carried out on the basis of the recommendations of the Report *The Canon Law of the Church of England*, published in 1947. The Canons printed here have all been promulged and have the force of law.

Canons are made by the Convocations (after 1970 by the General Synod) with the Royal Assent. In so far as they deal with matters not covered by the statute law (which includes Church Assembly Measures) they are binding *proprio vigore* on the clergy. For reasons of comprehensiveness and convenience, as well as to indicate that they possess spiritual authority, the present volume also contains a number of Canons which summarize or refer to certain statutory enactments. It does not contain Acts of Convocation, which, though they are solemn resolutions of the synods possessing a moral authority, do not have legal force.

From what has been already said, it will be obvious that this collection of Canons is not a complete statement of the law of the Church of England. It is, in fact, a revision of the Code of Canons issued in 1603 and covers roughly the same areas of church life, but like that Code it presupposes both the common and statute law of England and the general pre-Reformation Canon Law of the Western Church, except where that Canon Law has been affected by contrary statute or custom in England. In this it differs to some extent from the much more comprehensive Code of the Roman Catholic Church, and it follows the English secular legal tradition in its dislike of complete codification.

As part of the process of promulgation of the new Canons the Code of 1603 and other Canons made since then have been repealed, with two exceptions, about which something further must be said.

The first of these is the proviso to the old Canon 113. That Canon stated the duty of the parish priest to join with the church-wardens and other lay officers in presenting offenders to the bishop, and, the procedure of such presentation having been abandoned by the Church, the Canon itself has been repealed as obsolete. There was, however, a proviso excepting from the priest's duty matters revealed to him in confession and admonishing him, in general terms, not to disclose such matters. This was the only reference in post-Reformation Canon Law to the seal of confession. Since that reference was made in 1603, the modern law of evidence has developed in ways which raise difficulties about the enactment of a new Canon on the seal of confession. It has, therefore, been thought best to leave the proviso to the old Canon 113 unrepealed (see page 82). The adherence of the Church of England to the principle of the seal of confession has been stated in an Act of the Convocation of Canterbury passed in April 1959 in the following words:

> That this House reaffirms as an essential principle of Church doctrine that if any person confess his secret and hidden sin to a priest for the unburdening of his conscience, and to receive spiritual consolation and absolution from him, such priest is strictly charged that he do not at any time reveal or make known to any person whatsoever any sin so committed to his trust and secrecy.

The other Canon not now repealed is Canon 143, made in 1921. It concerns the membership of the Lower Houses of the two Convocations, and is at present under revision as part of the establishment of the new system of synodical government. There will eventually be added to the present Canons a section dealing with the synods of the Church, and it has been thought best to leave Canon 143 unrepealed until that is done.

In his Introduction to *The Canon Law of the Church of England* Dr Garbett, Archbishop of York, wrote: "At the present time the Church of England, alone among the Churches of the Anglican Communion, lacks a body of Canons which has been revised and supplemented in the light of modern conditions, and which is regarded as authoritative by its members.... This state of confusion and uncertainty is profoundly humiliating and unsatisfactory, and until it is remedied it will be difficult to secure order and cohesion in our Church." He added: "Through the very nature of the case there can be no final body of Canons. For a living Church will frequently desire both to amend existing Canons and to add to their number as new needs arise." For this reason at the conclusion of the recent revision there has been set up a Canon Law Standing Commission, whose duty it is to keep the Canon Law under review, to suggest changes when changed circumstances seem to call for them, and to draft such revisions and additions to the Canons as the legislative bodies of the Church may in due course desire. It is hoped that in this way the law of the Church can be prevented from again becoming stifling or obsolete and can be made to perform its proper function in the building up of the life of the Christian community.

MICHAEL CANTUAR:
DONALD EBOR:

May 1969

Section A

THE CHURCH OF ENGLAND

A 1　Of the Church of England

The Church of England, established according to the laws of this realm under the Queen's Majesty, belongs to the true and apostolic Church of Christ; and, as our duty to the said Church of England requires, we do constitute and ordain that no member thereof shall be at liberty to maintain or hold the contrary.

A 2　Of the Thirty-nine Articles of Religion

The Thirty-nine Articles are agreeable to the Word of God and may be assented unto with a good conscience by all members of the Church of England.

A 3　Of the Book of Common Prayer

1　The doctrine contained in *The Book of Common Prayer and Administration of the Sacraments and other Rites and Ceremonies of the Church according to the Use of the Church of England* is agreeable to the Word of God.

2　The form of God's worship contained in the said Book, forasmuch as it is not repugnant to the Word of God, may be used by all members of the Church of England with a good conscience.

A 4　Of the Form and Manner of Making, Ordaining, and Consecrating of Bishops, Priests, and Deacons

The Form and Manner of Making, Ordaining, and Consecrating of Bishops, Priests, and Deacons, annexed to the Book of Common Prayer and commonly known as the Ordinal, is not repugnant to the Word of God; and those who are so made, ordained, or consecrated bishops, priests, or deacons, according to the said Ordinal, are lawfully made, ordained, or consecrated, and ought to be accounted, both by themselves and others, to be truly bishops, priests, or deacons.

A 5　Of the doctrine of the Church of England

The doctrine of the Church of England is grounded in the holy Scriptures, and in such teachings of the ancient Fathers and Councils of the Church as are agreeable to the said Scriptures. In particular such doctrine is to be found in the Thirty-nine Articles of Religion, the Book of Common Prayer, and the Ordinal.

A 6   Of the government of the Church of England

The government of the Church of England under the Queen's Majesty, by archbishops, bishops, deans, provosts, archdeacons, and the rest of the clergy and of the laity that bear office in the same, is not repugnant to the Word of God.

A 7   Of the Royal Supremacy

We acknowledge that the Queen's most excellent Majesty, acting according to the laws of the realm, is the highest power under God in this kingdom, and has supreme authority over all persons in all causes, as well ecclesiastical as civil.

A 8   Of schisms

Forasmuch as the Church of Christ has for a long time past been distressed by separations and schisms among Christian men, so that the unity for which our Lord prayed is impaired and the witness to his gospel is grievously hindered, it is the duty of clergy and people to do their utmost not only to avoid occasions of strife but also to seek in penitence and brotherly charity to heal such divisions.

Section B

DIVINE SERVICE AND THE ADMINISTRATION OF THE SACRAMENTS

B 1 Of conformity to the Book of Common Prayer, except as may be ordered by lawful authority

1 Every minister shall follow the use and observe the orders, rites, and ceremonies prescribed in the Book of Common Prayer, as well in public prayer and reading of holy Scripture as in administration of the sacraments, and none other, except so far as shall be ordered by lawful authority.

2 The forms of service which are authorized by or under the four next following Canons or which are authorized or enjoined by the exercise of the powers or authorities set out in the next paragraph of this Canon shall be the forms of service which are ordered by lawful authority within the meaning of the Clerical Subscription Act, 1865; and any reference in this Canon or any other Canons to lawful authority shall be construed in like manner.

3 Nothing in the said Canons or this Canon shall prejudice or limit:

a the use of any form of service from time to time enjoined or authorized by any enactment or by Order in Council, Royal Warrant, or Royal Proclamation; or

b the powers of the bishop and the archbishop respectively to appease diversity and resolve doubts pursuant to the provision in the Book of Common Prayer entitled "Concerning the Service of the Church".

B 2 Of the approval of forms of service for experimental use

1 It shall be lawful for the Convocations of Canterbury and York to approve for experimental use within their respective provinces in any cathedral or church, or other place where the forms of service may be used, such forms of service alternative to the forms of service prescribed by the Book of Common Prayer and deviating (whether by way of addition, omission, substitution, or otherwise) from the forms of service so prescribed as in their opinion are neither contrary to, nor indicative of any departure from, the doctrine of the Church of England.

2 An approval of a form of service given under this Canon shall be required for each form of service and shall not have effect for

[7]

the purposes of this Canon unless the form of service is approved by both Convocations in the same terms with a majority in each House of each Convocation of not less than two-thirds of those present and voting, and is agreed to by the House of Laity with a majority of not less than two-thirds of those present and voting.

3   The periods during which such forms of service may be used, and the powers to renew and extend the periods and to revoke, vary, and replace the forms of service, shall be those prescribed by the Prayer Book (Alternative and Other Services) Measure, 1965.

4   A form of service approved under this Canon may not be used in any cathedral which is a parish church or in any church in a parish without the agreement of the parochial church council of the parish or in any guild church without the agreement of the guild church council, or in the case of services known as Occasional Offices if any of the persons concerned objects beforehand to its use.

B 3   Of the preliminary trial of draft services

1   For the purpose of giving a preliminary trial to a form of service which is under consideration by the Convocations of Canterbury and York with a view to approval being given thereto under Canon B 2, the said Convocations may approve a draft of the said form of service for use within their respective provinces for a period or periods of trial:

a   in any cathedral with the approval of the dean and the chapter or the cathedral chapter, as the case may be; and

b   subject to the control and supervision of the bishop of the diocese, in such church or churches, or other place or places where the relevant form of service prescribed by the Book of Common Prayer may be used, as he may arrange with the approval in each case of the incumbent of the benefice.

2   The times and periods at or during which such drafts of forms of service may be used, and the powers to revoke, vary, and replace the drafts, shall be those prescribed by the Prayer Book (Alternative and Other Services) Measure, 1965.

3   A draft of a form of service approved under this Canon may not be used in any cathedral which is a parish church or in any church in a parish without the agreement of the parochial church council of the parish or in any guild church without the agreement

of the guild church council, or in the case of services known as
Occasional Offices if any of the persons concerned objects beforehand to its use.

B 4   Of forms of service approved by the
Convocations or the Ordinary for use
on certain occasions

1   The Convocations of Canterbury and York may approve
within their respective provinces forms of service for use in any
cathedral or church or elsewhere on occasions for which no provision is made in the Book of Common Prayer, being forms of
service which in both words and order are in their opinion reverent
and seemly and neither contrary to, nor indicative of any departure
from, the doctrine of the Church of England.

2   The Ordinary, subject to any regulations made from time to
time by the Convocation of the province within which his jurisdiction lies, may approve for use in any cathedral or church or
elsewhere forms of service to meet circumstances for which no
provision is made in the Book of Common Prayer or by the Convocations under paragraph 1 of this Canon, being forms of service
which in the opinion of the Ordinary in both words and order are
reverent and seemly and are neither contrary to, nor indicative of
any departure from, the doctrine of the Church of England.

B 5   Of the discretion of the minister in conduct
of public prayer

1   The minister may in his discretion make and use variations
which are not of substantial importance in any form of service
prescribed by the Book of Common Prayer or authorized for use
under the four last foregoing Canons according to particular
circumstances.

2   Subject to any regulations made from time to time by the
Convocation of the province, the minister may on occasions for
which no provision is made in the Book of Common Prayer or
under the last preceding Canon use forms of service considered
suitable by him for those occasions.

3   All variations in forms of service and all forms of service used
or made under this Canon shall be reverent and seemly and shall

be neither contrary to, nor indicative of any departure from, the doctrine of the Church of England.

4   If any question is raised concerning the observance of the provisions of the last preceding paragraph or whether a variation in a form of service is of substantial importance or not, it may be referred to the bishop in order that he may give such pastoral guidance or advice as he may think fit, but such reference shall be without prejudice to the matter in question being made the subject-matter of proceedings under the Ecclesiastical Jurisdiction Measure, 1963.

B 6   Of Sundays and other days of special observance

1   The Lord's Day, commonly called Sunday, is ever to be celebrated as a weekly memorial of our Lord's resurrection and kept according to God's holy will and pleasure, particularly by attendance at divine service, by deeds of charity, and by abstention from all unnecessary labour and business.

2   The Table of Feasts which are to be observed in the Church of England is contained in the Book of Common Prayer; whereof the principal are Christmas Day, Epiphany, the Annunciation of the Blessed Virgin Mary, Easter Day, Ascension Day, Whitsunday, Trinity Sunday, and All Saints' Day.

3   The Days of Fasting or Abstinence and the Vigils which are to be observed in the Church of England are set out in the Book of Common Prayer, whereof the forty days of Lent, particularly Ash Wednesday and the Monday to Saturday before Easter, ought specially to be observed.

4   Good Friday is ever to be observed by prayer with meditation on the death and passion of our Lord and Saviour Jesus Christ, by self-discipline, and by attendance at divine service.

5   It is lawful for the Convocations of Canterbury and York to approve Holy Days which may be observed provincially, and, subject to any directions of the Convocation of the province, for the Ordinary to approve Holy Days which may be observed locally.

B 7   Of the giving notice of Feast Days and Fast Days

The minister shall give notice every Sunday publicly during the time of divine service, and by notice affixed at the church door or otherwise, so that the same may best be brought to the knowledge of the people, of the Feast Days and Fast Days which are to be observed in the week following, and of the times of the services thereon.

B 8   Of the vesture of ministers during the time of divine service

1   At Morning and Evening Prayer the minister shall wear a cassock, a surplice, and a scarf: and for the Occasional Offices a cassock and a surplice with scarf or stole.

2   At the Holy Communion the celebrant, as also the gospeller and the epistoler, if any, shall wear with the cassock either a surplice with scarf or stole, or a surplice or alb with stole and cope, or an alb with the customary vestments.

3   On any appropriate occasion a cope may be worn at the discretion of the minister.

4   When a scarf is worn, the minister may also wear the hood of his degree.

5   The Church of England does not attach any particular doctrinal significance to the diversities of vesture permitted by this Canon, and the vesture worn by the minister in accordance with the provisions of this Canon is not to be understood as implying any doctrines other than those now contained in the formularies of the Church of England.

6   Notwithstanding the foregoing provisions of this Canon no minister shall change the form of vesture in use in the church or chapel in which he officiates unless he has ascertained by consultation with the parochial church council that such changes will be acceptable: Provided always that in case of disagreement the minister shall refer the matter to the bishop of the diocese, whose direction shall be obeyed.

B 9   Of reverence and attention to be used in the time of divine service

1   All persons present in the time of divine service shall in the due places audibly with the minister say the General Confession, the Lord's Prayer, and the Creed, and make the answers appointed in the Book of Common Prayer.

2   They shall reverently kneel or stand when the prayers are read, and shall stand at the saying or singing of the Canticles and the Creed and at the reading of the holy Gospel, giving due reverence to the name of the Lord Jesus.

B 10   Of Morning and Evening Prayer in cathedral churches

In every cathedral church the Common Prayer shall be said or sung, distinctly, reverently, and in an audible voice, every morning and evening, and the Litany on the appointed days, the officiating ministers and others of the clergy present in choir being duly habited.

B 11   Of Morning and Evening Prayer in parish churches

1   In every parish church, except for some reasonable cause approved by the bishop of the diocese, Morning and Evening Prayer shall be said or sung at least on all Sundays and other principal Feast Days, and also on Ash Wednesday and Good Friday. Each service shall be said or sung distinctly, reverently, and in an audible voice.

2   Before authorizing the minister of the parish to dispense with either Morning or Evening Prayer on Sundays in the parish church for a period of more than three months, the bishop of the diocese shall consult with the parochial church council of the parish or two members thereof nominated by the council for that purpose.

3   On all other days the minister of the parish, together with all other ministers licensed to serve in the said parish, being at home and not otherwise reasonably hindered, shall resort to the church morning and evening, and, warning being given to the people by the tolling of the bell, say or sing the Common Prayers and on the appointed days the Litany.

4 Readers and such other lay persons as may be authorized by the bishop of the diocese may, at the invitation of the minister of the parish or, where the cure is vacant or the minister is incapacitated, at the invitation of the churchwardens, say or sing Morning or Evening Prayer (save for the Absolution); and in the case of need where no clerk in holy orders or reader or lay person authorized as aforesaid is available, the minister or (failing him) the churchwardens shall arrange for some suitable lay person to say or sing Morning or Evening Prayer (save for the Absolution).

B 12 Of the ministry of the Holy Communion

1 No person shall consecrate and administer the holy sacrament of the Lord's Supper unless he shall have been ordained priest by episcopal ordination in accordance with the provisions of Canon C 1.

2 Every minister, as often as he shall celebrate the Holy Communion, shall receive that sacrament himself.

3 No person shall distribute the holy sacrament of the Lord's Supper to the people unless he shall have been ordained in accordance with the provisions of Canon C 1, or unless he has been specially authorized to do so by the bishop acting under such regulations as the Convocations may make from time to time with the concurrence of the Church Assembly.

4 Subject to the general directions of the bishop, the Epistle and the Gospel may at the invitation of the minister be read by a lay person at the celebration of the Holy Communion.

B 13 Of Holy Communion in cathedral churches

1 In every cathedral church the Holy Communion shall be celebrated at least on all Sundays and other Feast Days, on Ash Wednesday, and on other days as often as may be convenient, according to the statutes and customs of each church. It shall be celebrated distinctly, reverently, and in an audible voice.

2 In every cathedral church the dean or provost, the canons residentiary, and the other ministers of the church, being in holy orders, shall all receive the Holy Communion every Sunday at the least, except they have a reasonable cause to the contrary.

B 14   Of Holy Communion in parish churches

1   In every parish church, except for some reasonable cause approved by the bishop of the diocese, the Holy Communion shall be celebrated at least on all Sundays and principal Feast Days, and on Ash Wednesday. It shall be celebrated distinctly, reverently, and in an audible voice.

2   In churches and chapels dependent on a parish church, the Holy Communion shall be celebrated as regularly and frequently as may be convenient, subject to the direction of the Ordinary.

B 15   Of the receiving of Holy Communion

1   It is the duty of all who have been confirmed to receive the Holy Communion regularly, and especially at the festivals of Christmas, Easter, and Whitsun.

2   The minister shall teach the people from time to time, and especially before the festivals of Christmas, Easter, and Whitsun, that they come to this holy sacrament with such preparation as is required by the Book of Common Prayer.

B 16   Of notorious offenders not to be admitted
to Holy Communion

1   If a minister be persuaded that anyone of his cure who presents himself to be a partaker of the Holy Communion ought not to be admitted thereunto by reason of malicious and open contention with his neighbours, or other grave and open sin without repentance, he shall give an account of the same to the bishop of the diocese or other the Ordinary of the place and therein obey his order and direction, but so as not to refuse the sacrament to any until in accordance with such order and direction he shall have called him and advertised him that in any wise he presume not to come to the Lord's table: Provided that in case of grave and immediate scandal to the congregation the minister shall not admit such person, but shall give an account of the same to the Ordinary within seven days after at the furthest and therein obey his order and direction. Provided also that before issuing his order and direction in relation to any such person the Ordinary shall afford to him an opportunity for interview.

2   The references in this Canon to "the bishop of the diocese or other the Ordinary of the place" and to "the Ordinary" include, in the case of the Ordinary being the bishop of the diocese and the see being vacant, the archbishop of the province or, in the case of the archbishopric being vacant or the vacant see being Canterbury or York, the archbishop of the other province.

B 17   Of bread and wine for the Holy Communion

1   The churchwardens of every parish, with the advice and direction of the minister, shall provide a sufficient quantity of bread and of wine for the number of communicants that shall from time to time receive the same.

2   The bread, whether leavened or unleavened, shall be of the best and purest wheat flour that conveniently may be gotten, and the wine the fermented juice of the grape, good and wholesome.

3   The bread shall be brought to the communion table in a paten or convenient box and the wine in a convenient cruet or flagon.

B 18   Of sermons in parish churches

1   In every parish church a sermon shall be preached at least once each Sunday, except for some reasonable cause approved by the bishop of the diocese.

2   The preacher shall endeavour himself with care and sincerity to minister the word of truth, to the glory of God and to the edification of the people.

B 19   Of the Bidding Prayer which may be used by a preacher before his sermon

Before any sermon, lecture, or homily, the preacher may move the people to join with him in prayer in this form or to this effect, as briefly as is convenient, always concluding with the Lord's Prayer:

Ye shall pray for Christ's holy Catholic Church, that is, for the whole congregation of Christian people dispersed throughout the whole world, and especially for the Church of England.

And herein I require you most especially to pray for the Queen's most excellent Majesty our Sovereign Lady Elizabeth, by the grace of God of the United Kingdom of Great Britain and Northern Ireland, and of her other realms and territories, Queen, Head of the Commonwealth, Defender of the Faith, and ye shall also pray for Elizabeth the Queen Mother, Philip Duke of Edinburgh, Charles Prince of Wales, and all the Royal Family.

Ye shall also pray for the ministers of God's holy word and sacraments, as well archbishops and bishops, as other pastors and curates; for the Queen's most honourable Privy Council and the Ministers of the Crown, for the High Court of Parliament, for the Convocations of the Clergy, for the National Assembly of the Church of England, and for civil governors and magistrates; that all and every of these, in their several callings, may serve truly and diligently, to the glory of God and the edifying and well governing of her people, remembering the strict and solemn account that they must one day make when they shall stand before the judgement seat of Christ.

And, that there may never be wanting a succession of persons duly qualified to serve God in Church and State, ye shall implore his blessing on all places of religious and useful learning, particularly the universities, colleges, and schools of this land; that in all places of education true religion and sound learning may for ever flourish and abound.

And more particularly (as in private duty bound) I ask your prayers for...

Also ye shall pray for the whole people of this realm, that they may live in the true faith and fear of God, in dutiful obedience to the Queen, and in brotherly charity one to another.

Finally, let us praise God for all those who are departed out of this life in the faith of Christ, and pray unto God that we may have grace to direct our lives after their good example; that, this life ended, we may be made partakers with them of the glorious resurrection in the life everlasting.

B 20   Of the hymns, anthems, and music of the Church

1   In all churches and chapels, other than in cathedral or collegiate churches or chapels where the matter is governed by or dependent upon the statutes or customs of the same, it belongs to the minister to direct when the organ shall be played and when it shall not be played, and to decide what parts of the service shall be sung.

2   Where there is an organist or choirmaster the minister shall pay due heed to his advice and assistance in the choosing of chants,

hymns, anthems, and other settings and in the ordering of the music of the Church; but at all times the final responsibility and decision in these matters rests with the minister.

3 It is the duty of the minister to ensure that only such chants, hymns, anthems, and other settings are chosen as are appropriate, both the words and the music, to the solemn act of worship and prayer in the House of God as well as to the congregation assembled for that purpose; and to banish all irreverence in the practice and in the performance of the same.

B 21 Of Holy Baptism

It is desirable that every minister having a cure of souls shall from time to time administer the sacrament of Holy Baptism upon Sundays or other Holy Days at or immediately after public worship when the most number of people come together, that the congregation there present may witness the receiving of them that be newly baptized into Christ's Church, and be put in remembrance of their own profession made to God in their baptism. Nevertheless (if necessity so require) children may be baptized on any other day.

B 22 Of the baptism of infants

1 Due notice, normally of at least a week, shall be given before a child is brought to the church to be baptized.

2 If the minister shall refuse or unduly delay to baptize any such infant, the parents or guardians may apply to the bishop of the diocese, who shall, after consultation with the minister, give such directions as he thinks fit.

3 The minister shall instruct the parents or guardians of an infant to be admitted to Holy Baptism that the same responsibilities rest on them as are in the service of Holy Baptism required of the godparents.

4 No minister shall refuse or, save for the purpose of preparing or instructing the parents or guardians or godparents, delay to baptize any infant within his cure that is brought to the church to be baptized, provided that due notice has been given and the provisions relating to godparents in these Canons are observed.

5 A minister who intends to baptize any infant whose parents
are residing outside the boundaries of his cure, unless the names of
such persons or of one of them be on the church electoral roll of
the same, shall not proceed to the baptism without having sought
the good will of the minister of the parish in which such parents
reside.

6 No minister being informed of the weakness or danger of
death of any infant within his cure and therefore desired to go to
baptize the same shall either refuse or delay to do so.

7 A minister so baptizing a child in a hospital or nursing home,
the parents of the child not being resident in his cure, nor their
names on the church electoral roll of the same, shall send their
names and address to the minister of the parish in which they
reside.

8 If any infant which is privately baptized do afterwards live,
it shall be brought to the church and there, by the minister, received
into the congregation of Christ's flock according to the form and
manner prescribed in and by the office for Private Baptism in the
Book of Common Prayer.

9 The minister of every parish shall warn the people that without
grave cause and necessity they should not have their children baptized privately in their houses.

B 23   Of godparents and sponsors

1 For every child to be baptized there shall be not fewer than
three godparents, of whom at least two shall be of the same sex as
the child and of whom at least one shall be of the opposite sex; save
that, when three cannot conveniently be had, one godfather and
godmother shall suffice. Parents may be godparents for their own
children provided that the child have at least one other godparent.

2 The godparents shall be persons who will faithfully fulfil their
responsibilities both by their care for the children committed to
their charge and by the example of their own godly living.

3 When one who is of riper years is to be baptized he shall
choose three, or at least two, to be his sponsors, who shall be ready
to present him at the font and afterwards put him in mind of his
Christian profession and duties.

4 No person shall be admitted to be a sponsor or godparent who has not been baptized and confirmed. Nevertheless the minister shall have power to dispense with the requirement of confirmation in any case in which in his judgement need so requires.

B 24   Of the baptism of such as are of riper years

1 When any such person as is of riper years and able to answer for himself is to be baptized, the minister shall instruct such person, or cause him to be instructed, in the principles of the Christian religion, and exhort him so to prepare himself with prayers and fasting that he may receive this holy sacrament with repentance and faith.

2 At least a week before any such baptism is to take place, the minister shall give notice thereof to the bishop of the diocese or whomsoever he shall appoint for the purpose.

3 Every person thus baptized shall be confirmed by the bishop so soon after his baptism as conveniently may be; that so he may be admitted to the Holy Communion.

B 25   Of the sign of the Cross in baptism

The Church of England has ever held and taught, and holds and teaches still, that the sign of the Cross used in baptism is no part of the substance of the sacrament: but, for the remembrance of the Cross, which is very precious to those that rightly believe in Jesus Christ, has retained the sign of it in baptism, following therein the primitive and apostolic Churches.

B 26   Of teaching the young

1 Every minister shall take care that the children and young people within his cure are instructed in the doctrine, sacraments, and discipline of Christ, as the Lord has commanded and as they are set forth in the holy Scriptures, in the Book of Common Prayer, and especially in the Church Catechism; and to this end he, or some godly and competent persons appointed by him, shall on Sundays or if need be at other convenient times diligently instruct and teach them in the same.

2 All parents and guardians shall take care that their children receive such instruction.

B 27   Of confirmation

1   The bishop of every diocese shall himself minister (or cause to
be ministered by some other bishop lawfully deputed in his stead)
the rite of confirmation throughout his diocese as often and in as
many places as shall be convenient, laying his hands upon children
and other persons who have been baptized and instructed in the
Christian faith.

2   Every minister who has a cure of souls shall diligently seek
out children and other persons whom he shall think meet to be
confirmed and shall use his best endeavour to instruct them in the
Christian faith and life as set forth in the holy Scriptures, the Book
of Common Prayer, and the Church Catechism contained therein.

3   The minister shall present none to the bishop but such as are
come to years of discretion and can say the Creed, the Lord's
Prayer, and the Ten Commandments, and can also render an account of their faith according to the said Catechism.

4   The minister shall satisfy himself that those whom he is to
present have been validly baptized, ascertaining the date and place
of such baptism, and, before or at the time assigned for the confirmation, shall give to the bishop their names, together with their
age and the date of their baptism.

5   If the minister is doubtful about the baptism of a candidate
for confirmation he shall conditionally baptize him according to the
form and manner prescribed in the Book of Common Prayer before
presenting him to the bishop to be confirmed.

6   If it is desired for sufficient reason that a Christian name be
changed, the bishop may, under the laws of this realm, confirm a
person by a new Christian name, which shall be thereafter deemed
the lawful Christian name of such person.

B 28   Of reception into the Church of England

1   Any person desiring to be received into the Church of England,
who has not been baptized or the validity of whose baptism can be
held in question, shall be instructed and baptized or conditionally
baptized, and such baptism, or conditional baptism, shall constitute
the said person's reception into the Church of England.

2 If any such person has been baptized but not episcopally confirmed and desires to be formally admitted into the Church of England he shall, after appropriate instruction, be received by the rite of confirmation, or, if he be not yet ready to be presented for confirmation, he shall be received by the parish priest with appropriate prayers.

3 If any such person has been episcopally confirmed with unction or with the laying on of hands he shall be instructed, and, with the permission of the bishop, received into the Church of England according to the Form of Reception approved by Convocation, or with other appropriate prayers, and if any such person be a priest he shall be received into the said Church only by the bishop of the diocese or by the commissary of such bishop.

B 29   Of the ministry of absolution*

1 It is the duty of baptized persons at all times to the best of their understanding to examine their lives and conversations by the rule of God's commandments, and whereinsoever they perceive themselves to have offended by will, act, or omission, there to bewail their own sinfulness and to confess themselves to Almighty God with full purpose of amendment of life, that they may receive of him the forgiveness of sins which he has promised to all who turn to him with hearty repentance and true faith; acknowledging their sins and seeking forgiveness, especially in the general Confessions of the congregation and in the Absolutions pronounced by the priest in the services of the Church.

2 If there be any who by these means cannot quiet his own conscience, but requires further comfort or counsel, let him come to some discreet and learned minister of God's Word; that by the ministry of God's holy Word he may receive the benefit of absolution, together with ghostly counsel and advice, to the quieting of his conscience and avoiding of all scruple and doubtfulness.

3 In particular a sick person, if he feels his conscience troubled in any weighty matter, should make a special confession of his sins, that the priest may absolve him if he humbly and heartily desire it.

4 No priest shall exercise the ministry of absolution in any place without the permission of the minister having the cure of souls

* See also the unrepealed proviso to Canon 113 of the Code of 1603 (p. 82).

thereof, unless he is by law authorized to exercise his ministry in that place without being subject to the control of the minister having the general cure of souls of the parish or district in which it is situated: Provided always that, notwithstanding the foregoing provisions of this Canon, a priest may exercise the ministry of absolution anywhere in respect of any person who is in danger of death or if there is some urgent or weighty cause.

B 30 Of Holy Matrimony

1   The Church of England affirms, according to our Lord's teaching, that marriage is in its nature a union permanent and life-long, for better for worse, till death them do part, of one man with one woman, to the exclusion of all others on either side, for the procreation and nurture of children, for the hallowing and right direction of the natural instincts and affections, and for the mutual society, help, and comfort which the one ought to have of the other, both in prosperity and adversity.

2   The teaching of our Lord affirmed by the Church of England is expressed and maintained in the Form of Solemnization of Matrimony contained in the Book of Common Prayer.

3   It shall be the duty of the minister, when application is made to him for matrimony to be solemnized in the church of which he is the minister, to explain to the two persons who desire to be married the Church's doctrine of marriage as herein set forth, and the need of God's grace in order that they may discharge aright their obligations as married persons.

B 31 Of certain impediments to marriage

1   No person who is under sixteen years of age shall marry, and all marriages purported to be made between persons either of whom is under sixteen years of age are void.

2   No person shall marry within the degrees expressed in the following Table, and all marriages purported to be made within the said degrees are void.

A TABLE OF KINDRED AND AFFINITY

A man may not marry his	*A woman may not marry with her*
mother	father
daughter	son
adopted daughter	adopted son
father's mother	father's father
mother's mother	mother's father
son's daughter	son's son
daughter's daughter	daughter's son
sister	brother
wife's mother	husband's father
wife's daughter	husband's son
father's wife	mother's husband
son's wife	daughter's husband
father's father's wife	father's mother's husband
mother's father's wife	mother's mother's husband
wife's father's mother	husband's father's father
wife's mother's mother	husband's mother's father
wife's daughter's daughter	husband's son's son
wife's son's daughter	husband's daughter's son
son's son's wife	son's daughter's husband
daughter's son's wife	daughter's daughter's husband
father's sister	father's brother
mother's sister	mother's brother
brother's daughter	brother's son
sister's daughter	sister's son

In this Table the term "brother" includes a brother of the half-blood, and the term "sister" includes a sister of the half-blood.

This Table shall be in every church publicly set up and fixed at the charge of the parish.

B 32   Of certain impediments to the solemnization of matrimony

No minister shall solemnize matrimony between two persons either of whom (not being a widow or widower) is under twenty-one years of age otherwise than in accordance with the requirements of the law relating to the consent of parents or guardians in the case of the marriage of a person under twenty-one years of age.

B 33   Of the duty of the minister to inquire as to impediments

It shall be the duty of the minister, when application is made to him for matrimony to be solemnized in the church or chapel of which he is the minister, to inquire whether there be any impediment either to the marriage or to the solemnization thereof.

B 34   Of requirements preliminary to the solemnization of matrimony

1   A marriage according to the rites of the Church of England may be solemnized:

a   after the publication of banns of marriage;

b   on the authority of a special licence of marriage granted by the Archbishop of Canterbury or any other person by virtue of the Ecclesiastical Licences Act, 1533 (in these Canons, and in the statute law, referred to as a "special licence");

c   on the authority of a licence (other than a special licence) granted by an ecclesiastical authority having power to grant such a licence (in these Canons, and in the statute law, referred to as a "common licence"); or

d   on the authority of a certificate issued by a superintendent registrar under the provisions of the statute law in that behalf.

2   The Archbishop of Canterbury may grant a special licence for the solemnization of matrimony without the publication of banns at any convenient time or place not only within the province of Canterbury but throughout all England.

3   The archbishop of each province, the bishop of every diocese, and all others who of ancient right have been accustomed to issue a common licence may grant such a licence for the solemnization of matrimony without the publication of banns at a lawful time and in a lawful place within the several areas of their jurisdiction as the case may be; and the Archbishop of Canterbury may grant a common licence for the same throughout all England.

B 35   Of rules to be observed as to the preliminaries and to the solemnization of Holy Matrimony

1   In all matters pertaining to the granting of licences of marriage every ecclesiastical authority shall observe the law relating thereto.

2   In all matters pertaining to the publication of banns of marriage and to the solemnization of matrimony every minister shall observe the law relating thereto, including, so far as they are applicable, the rules prescribed by the rubric prefixed to the office of Solemnization of Matrimony in the Book of Common Prayer.

3   A marriage may not be solemnized at any unseasonable hours but only between the hours of eight in the forenoon and six in the afternoon.

4   Every marriage shall be solemnized in the presence of two or more witnesses besides the minister who shall solemnize the same.

5   When matrimony is to be solemnized in any church, it belongs to the minister of the parish to decide what music shall be played, what hymns or anthems shall be sung, or what furnishings or flowers should be placed in or about the church for the occasion.

B 36   Of a service after civil marriage

1   If any persons have contracted marriage before the civil registrar under the provisions of the statute law, and shall afterwards desire to add thereto a service of Solemnization of Matrimony, a minister may, if he see fit, use such form of service, as may be sanctioned by lawful authority, in the church or chapel in which he is authorized to exercise his ministry: Provided first, that the minister be duly certified that the civil marriage has been contracted, and secondly that in regard to this use of the said service the minister do observe the Canons and regulations of the Convocations for the time being in force.

2   In connection with such a service there shall be no publication of banns nor any licence or certificate authorizing a marriage: and no record of any such service shall be entered by the minister in the register books of marriages provided by the Registrar General.

B 37   Of the ministry to the sick

1   The minister shall use his best endeavours to ensure that he be speedily informed when any person is sick or in danger of death in the parish, and shall as soon as possible resort unto him to exhort, instruct, and comfort him in his distress in such manner as he shall think most needful and convenient.

2   When any person sick or in danger of death or so impotent that he cannot go to church is desirous of receiving the most comfortable sacrament of the Body and Blood of Christ, the priest, having knowledge thereof, shall as soon as may be visit him, and unless there be any grave reason to the contrary, shall reverently minister the same to the said person at such place and time as may be convenient.

3   If any such person so desires, the priest may lay hands upon him and may anoint him with oil on the forehead with the sign of the Cross using the form of service sanctioned by lawful authority and using pure olive oil consecrated by the bishop of the diocese or otherwise by the priest himself in accordance with such form of service.

B 38   Of the burial of the dead

1   In all matters pertaining to the burial of the dead every minister shall observe the law from time to time in force in relation thereto, and, subject to this paragraph in general, the following paragraphs of this Canon shall be obeyed.

2   No minister shall refuse to bury, according to the rites of the Church of England, the corpse or ashes of any person deceased within his cure or of any parishioner whether deceased within his cure or elsewhere that is brought to a church or burial ground or cemetery under his control in which the burial or interment of such corpse or ashes may lawfully be effected, due notice being given; except the person deceased have died unbaptized, or being of sound mind have laid violent hands upon himself, or have been declared excommunicate for some grievous and notorious crime and no man to testify to his repentance; in which case and in any other case at the request of the relative, friend, or legal representative having charge of or being responsible for the burial he shall use at the burial such service as may be prescribed or approved by the Ordinary, being a service neither contrary to, nor indicative of any departure from, the doctrine of the Church of England: Provided

that, if a form of service available for the burial of suicides is approved under Section 4 of the Prayer Book (Alternative and Other Services) Measure, 1965, that service shall be used where applicable instead of the aforesaid service prescribed or approved by the Ordinary, unless the person having charge or being responsible for the burial otherwise requests.

3   Cremation of a dead body is lawful in connection with Christian burial.

4   *a*   When a body is to be cremated, the burial service may precede, accompany, or follow the cremation; and may be held either in the church or at the crematorium: Provided that no incumbent shall be under any obligation to perform a funeral service within the grounds of any burial authority, but, on his refusal so to do, any clerk in holy orders, not being prohibited under ecclesiastical censure, may, with the permission of the bishop and at the request of the person having charge of the cremation or interment of the cremated remains, perform such service within such grounds.

    b   Save for good and sufficient reason the ashes of a cremated body should be interred or deposited, by a minister, in consecrated ground.

5   When a body is to be buried according to the rites of the Church of England in any unconsecrated ground, the officiating minister, on coming to the grave, shall first bless the same.

6   If any doubt shall arise whether any person deceased may be buried according to the rites of the Church of England, the minister shall refer the matter to the bishop and obey his order and direction.

B 39   Of the registration of baptisms, confirmations, marriages, and burials

1   In all matters pertaining to the registration of baptisms, marriages, and burials every minister shall observe the law from time to time in force relating thereto.

2   When any person is presented for confirmation, the minister presenting the said person shall record and enter the confirmation in his register book of confirmations provided in accordance with paragraph 3 of Canon F 11, together with any change of name made under paragraph 6 of Canon B 27.

B 40 Of Holy Communion elsewhere than in consecrated buildings

No minister shall celebrate the Holy Communion elsewhere than in a consecrated building within his cure or other building licensed for the purpose, except he have permission so to do from the bishop of the diocese: Provided that at all times he may celebrate the Holy Communion as provided by Canon B 37 in any private house wherein there is any person sick, or dying, or so impotent that he cannot go to church.

B 41 Of divine service in private chapels

1   No chaplain, ministering in any house where there is a chapel dedicated and allowed by the ecclesiastical laws of this realm, shall celebrate the Holy Communion in any other part of the house but in such chapel, and shall do the same seldom upon Sunday and other greater Feast Days, so that the residents in the said house may resort to their parish church and there attend divine service.

2   The bishop of a diocese within which any college, school, hospital, or public or charitable institution is situated, whether or not it possesses a chapel, may license a minister to perform such offices and services of the Church of England (except the solemnization of marriages) as may be specified in the licence on any premises forming part of or belonging to the institution in question.

3   The performance of offices and services in accordance with any such licence shall not require the consent or be subject to the control of the minister of the parish in which they are performed.

B 42 Of the language of divine service

The Morning and Evening Prayer, and all other prayers and services prescribed in and by the Book of Common Prayer, shall be said or sung in the vulgar tongue, save that they may be lawfully said or sung in the Latin tongue in the Convocation of the province, in the chapels or other public places of the several colleges and halls in the universities, or in the university churches in the same, in the colleges of Westminster, Winchester, and Eton, and in such other places of religious and sound learning as custom allows or the bishop or other the Ordinary may permit.

Section C

MINISTERS, THEIR ORDINATION, FUNCTION, AND CHARGE

C 1 Of holy orders in the Church of England

1 The Church of England holds and teaches that from the Apostles' time there have been these orders in Christ's Church: bishops, priests, and deacons; and no man shall be accounted or taken to be a lawful bishop, priest, or deacon in the Church of England, or suffered to execute any of the said offices, except he be called, tried, examined, and admitted thereunto according to the Ordinal or any form of service alternative thereto ordered by lawful authority or has had formerly episcopal consecration or ordination in some Church whose orders are recognized and accepted by the Church of England.

2 No person who has been admitted to the order of bishop, priest, or deacon can ever be divested of the character of his order, but a minister may either by legal process voluntarily relinquish the exercise of his orders and use himself as a layman, or may by legal and canonical process be deprived of the exercise of his orders or deposed finally therefrom.

3 According to the ancient law and usage of this Church and Realm of England, the inferior clergy who have received authority to minister in any diocese owe canonical obedience in all things lawful and honest to the bishop of the same, and the bishop of each diocese owes due allegiance to the archbishop of the province as his metropolitan.

C 2 Of the consecration of bishops

1 No person shall be consecrated to the office of bishop by fewer than three bishops present together and joining in the act of consecration, of whom one shall be the archbishop of the province or a bishop appointed to act on his behalf.

2 The consecration of a bishop shall take place upon some Sunday or Holy Day, unless the archbishop, for urgent and weighty cause, shall appoint some other day.

3 No person shall be consecrated bishop except he shall be at least thirty years of age.

4 No person shall be refused consecration as bishop on the ground that he was born out of lawful wedlock.

C 3   Of the ordination of priests and deacons

1   Ordination to the office of priest or deacon shall take place upon the Sundays immediately following the Ember Weeks, or upon Michaelmas Day or St Thomas's Day, unless the bishop of the diocese on urgent occasion shall appoint some other day, being a Sunday, a Holy Day, or one of the Ember Days.

2   Ordinations of priests and deacons shall be in the cathedral church of the diocese, or other church or chapel at the discretion of the bishop.

3   One of the archdeacons, or his deputy, or such other persons as by ancient custom have the right so to do, shall present to the bishop every person who is to be ordained.

4   The priests taking part in an ordination shall together with the bishop lay their hands upon the head of every person who receives the order of priesthood.

5   No person shall be made deacon, except he be at least twenty-three years of age, unless he have a faculty from the Archbishop of Canterbury.

6   No person shall be ordained priest, except he be at least twenty-four years of age, unless being over the age of twenty-three he have a faculty from the Archbishop of Canterbury.

7   No person shall be ordained both deacon and priest upon one and the same day, unless he have a faculty from the Archbishop of Canterbury.

8   A deacon shall not be ordained to the priesthood for at least one year, unless the bishop shall find good cause for the contrary, so that trial may be made of his behaviour in the office of deacon before he be admitted to the order of priesthood. During a vacancy of the see, the power of the bishop under this paragraph shall be exercisable by the archbishop of the province in which the diocese is situate.

C 4   Of the quality of such as are to be ordained deacons or priests

1   Every bishop shall take care that he admit no person into holy orders but such as he knows either by himself, or by sufficient testimony, to have been baptized and confirmed, to be sufficiently instructed in holy Scripture and in the doctrine, discipline, and worship of the Church of England, and to be of virtuous conversation and good repute and such as to be a wholesome example and pattern to the flock of Christ.

2   No person shall be admitted into holy orders who is suffering, or who has suffered, from any physical or mental infirmity which in the opinion of the bishop will prevent him from ministering the word and sacraments or from performing the other duties of the minister's office.

3   No person shall be admitted into holy orders who has re-married and, the wife of that marriage being alive, has a former wife still living; or who is married to a person who has been previously married and whose former husband is still living.

4   No person shall be refused ordination as deacon or priest on the ground that he was born out of lawful wedlock.

C 5   Of the titles of such as are to be ordained deacons or priests

1   Any person to be admitted into holy orders shall first exhibit to the bishop of the diocese of whom he desires imposition of hands a certificate that he is provided of some ecclesiastical office within such diocese, which the bishop shall judge sufficient, wherein he may attend the cure of souls and execute his ministry.

2   A bishop may also admit into holy orders

a   any person holding office in any university, or any fellow, or any person in right as a fellow, in any college or hall in the same;

b   any master in a school;

c   any person who is to be a chaplain in any university or in any college or hall in the same or in any school;

d   any person who is to be a member of the staff of a theological college;

e any person who is living under vows in the house of any religious order or community:

Provided that the said university, college, hall, school, or house of a religious order or community be situate within his diocese.

3   A bishop may also admit into holy orders persons for service overseas in accordance with the statutory provisions in that behalf in force from time to time.

4   No person shall be admitted into holy orders by any bishop other than the bishop of the diocese in which he is to exercise his ministry, except he shall bring with him Letters Dimissory from the bishop of such diocese.

5   Notwithstanding any provision of the preceding paragraphs of this Canon, the ancient privilege of any fellow or any person in right as a fellow in any college or hall in the University of Oxford or of Cambridge to be admitted into holy orders without Letters Dimissory by any bishop willing to ordain him shall be unimpaired.

C 6   Of the certificates and Letters Testimonial to be exhibited to the bishop by such as are to be ordained deacons or priests

1   Every person who is to be made a deacon shall exhibit to the bishop of the diocese:

a a certificate or other sufficient evidence of the date and place of his birth;

b a certificate or other evidence of his baptism and confirmation;

c a certificate signed by the officiating minister and a church-warden of the parish in which he usually resides or in which his name is entered on the church electoral roll, certifying that the form commonly called *Si Quis* was read in the time of divine service on some Sunday at least a week before the day of ordination and that no impediment was alleged;

d Letters Testimonial of his good life and conversation from three priests, of whom one at least must be beneficed, who have had personal knowledge of his life and doctrine by the space of three years next before or of such time as shall satisfy the bishop; whose signatures shall be countersigned by the bishop of the diocese wherein the said priests are respectively either beneficed or licensed, if he be other than the bishop to whom the said letters are addressed;

e   if he shall have resided in any college or hall in any university, or in any theological college, similar Letters Testimonial from each such college or hall.

2   Every deacon who is to be ordained priest shall exhibit to the bishop of the diocese:

a   his Letters of Orders;
b   a certificate signed by the officiating minister and a church-warden of the parish or ecclesiastical district wherein he serves as a stipendiary curate or, if he be not such, wherein he usually resides, that the form *Si Quis* was read according to the provisions of paragraph 1 of this Canon and that no impediment was alleged;
c   Letters Testimonial of his good life and conversation from three priests, of whom one at least must be beneficed, who have had personal knowledge of his life, work, and doctrine during his diaconate; whose signatures shall be countersigned according to the provisions of paragraph 1 of this Canon.

3   When any person is to be ordained deacon or priest who is a fellow in any college or hall in any university, or a master in any school having a chapel belonging thereto, the form *Si Quis* may, with the consent in writing of the bishop who is to ordain him, be read in such chapel and the certificate signed by the officiating minister and the head of the college or hall, or the headmaster of the school, as the case may be.

C 7   Of examination for holy orders

No bishop shall admit any person into holy orders, except such person on careful and diligent examination, wherein the bishop shall have called to his assistance the archdeacons and other ministers appointed for this purpose, be found to possess a sufficient knowledge of holy Scripture and of the doctrine, discipline, and worship of the Church of England as set forth in the Thirty-nine Articles of Religion, the Book of Common Prayer, and the Ordinal; and to fulfil the requirements as to learning and other qualities which, subject to any directions given by the Convocation of the province, the bishop deems necessary for the office of deacon.

C 8   Of ministers exercising their ministry

1   Every minister shall exercise his ministry in accordance with the provisions of this Canon.

2   A minister duly ordained priest or deacon, and, where it is required under paragraph 5 of this Canon, holding a licence or permission from the archbishop of the province, may officiate in any place only after he has received authority to do so from the bishop of the diocese or other the Ordinary of the place.

Save that:

a   The minister having the cure of souls of a church or chapel or the sequestrator when the cure is vacant or the dean or provost and the canons residentiary of any cathedral or collegiate church may allow a minister, concerning whom they are satisfied either by actual personal knowledge or by good and sufficient evidence that he is of good life and standing and otherwise qualified under this Canon, to minister within their church or chapel for a period of not more than seven days within three months without reference to the bishop or other Ordinary, and a minister so allowed shall be required to sign the services register when he officiates.

b   No member of the chapter of a cathedral church shall be debarred from performing the duties of his office in due course and exercising his ministry within the diocese merely by lack of authority from the bishop of the diocese within which the cathedral is situate.

c   Any minister who has a licence to preach throughout the province from the archbishop or throughout England from the University of Oxford or of Cambridge, may preach the Word of God in any diocese within that province or throughout England, as the case may be, without any further authority from the bishop thereof.

3   The bishop of a diocese confers such authority on a minister either by instituting him to a benefice, or by admitting him to serve within his diocese by licence under his hand and seal, or by giving him written permission to officiate within the same.

4   No minister who has such authority to exercise his ministry in any diocese shall do so therein in any place in which he has not the cure of souls without the permission of the minister having such cure, except at the homes of persons whose names are entered on the electoral roll of the parish which he serves and to the extent

authorized by the Extra-Parochial Ministry Measure, 1967, or in a university, college, school, hospital, or public or charitable institution in which he is licensed to officiate as provided by the said Measure and Canon B 41.

5   A minister who has been ordained priest or deacon

a   by an overseas bishop within the meaning of the Overseas and Other Clergy (Ministry and Ordination) Measure, 1967;

b   under section 5 of that Measure for ministry overseas;

c   by a bishop in a Church not in communion with the Church of England, whose orders are recognized or accepted by the Church of England;

may not minister in the province of Canterbury or York without the permission of the archbishop of the province in question under the said Measure: Provided that this paragraph shall not apply to any person ordained priest or deacon by any such bishop on the request and by the commission in writing of the bishop of a diocese in the province of Canterbury or York.

C 9   Of collation and presentation

1   A vacancy or impending vacancy in any benefice shall be notified by the bishop of the diocese to the patron and to the parochial church council, and the provisions of the law from time to time in force relating to the filling of such vacancy shall be complied with.

2   Every bishop shall have twenty-eight days' space to inquire and inform himself of the sufficiency and qualities of every minister, after he has been presented to him to be instituted to any benefice.

C 10   Of admission and institution

1   No person shall be admitted or instituted to any benefice before such time as he shall have been ordained priest by episcopal ordination in accordance with the provisions of Canon C 1.

2   No bishop shall admit or institute to a benefice any priest who has been ordained by any other bishop, except such priest first show unto him his Letters of Orders or other sufficient evidence that he has been ordained, and bring him sufficient testimony, if the bishop shall require it, of his former good life and behaviour; and lastly, shall appear on due examination to be of sufficient learning.

3 A bishop may refuse to admit or institute any priest to a benefice

a if, at the date of the vacancy, not more than one year has elapsed since a transfer, as defined by the first section of the Benefices Act, 1898, of the right of patronage of the benefice, unless it be proved that the transfer was not effected in view of the probability of a vacancy within such year, or

b on the ground that at the date of presentation not more than three years have elapsed since the priest who has been presented to him was ordained deacon, or that the said priest is unfit for the discharge of the duties of a benefice by reason of physical or mental infirmity or incapacity, pecuniary embarrassment of a serious character, grave misconduct or neglect of duty in an ecclesiastical office, evil life, having by his conduct caused grave scandal concerning his moral character since his ordination, or having, with reference to the presentation, been knowingly party or privy to any transaction or agreement which is invalid under the Benefices Act, 1898.

4 No bishop shall admit or institute any priest to a benefice until the expiration of one month after notice, in the prescribed manner, that he proposes to institute such priest has been served on the churchwardens of the parish; which notice shall be published by the churchwardens in the prescribed manner.

5 After the expiration of one month from the serving of such notice on the churchwardens of the parish, the bishop shall, as speedily as may be, proceed to give institution to the priest to whom he has collated the benefice, or who has been presented to him to be instituted thereto, in accordance with the laws and statutes in that behalf provided; which institution he shall use his best endeavour to give in the parish church of the benefice.

6 The bishop, when he gives institution, shall read the words of institution from a written instrument having the episcopal seal appended thereto; and during the reading thereof the priest who is to be instituted shall kneel before the bishop and hold the seal in his hand.

7 If the bishop for some grave and urgent cause be unable to give institution himself he shall delegate power to some commissary in holy orders to give the same on his behalf.

8   The provisions of this Canon are without prejudice to the right of a patron or a presentee to appeal, in accordance with the laws of this realm, against the refusal of the bishop to institute.

C 11   Of induction

1   The bishop, after giving institution to any priest, shall issue Letters Mandatory for induction directed to the archdeacon or other the person to whom induction belongs, who shall thereupon induct the said priest into possession of the temporalities of the benefice.

2   The archdeacon or other such person, when he makes the induction, shall take the priest who is to be inducted by the hand and lay it upon the key or upon the ring of the church door, or if the key cannot be had and there is no ring on the door, or if the church be in ruins, upon any part of the wall of the church or churchyard, at the same time reading the words of induction; after which the priest who has been inducted shall toll the bell to make his induction public and known to the people.

3   If the archdeacon be unable to make the induction himself, he shall issue the accustomed mandate to all and singular ministers beneficed or licensed within his archdeaconry, by virtue of which any one such minister may make the induction on his behalf.

C 12   Of the licensing of ministers under seal

1   A licence, granted by a bishop under his hand and seal to any minister to serve within his diocese, shall be in the form either

a   of a general licence to preach or otherwise to minister subject to the provisions of paragraph 4 of Canon C 8 in any parish or ecclesiastical district, or
b   of a licence to perform some particular office.

2   No bishop shall grant any such licence to any minister who has come from another diocese, except such minister first show unto him Letters of Orders or other sufficient evidence that he is ordained, and bring him testimony, from the bishop of the diocese whence he has come, of his honesty, ability, and conformity to the doctrine, discipline, and worship of the Church of England, together with Letters Testimonial of his good life and conversation from three priests who are beneficed in the said diocese, countersigned by the bishop of the same.

3   Every minister who is to be licensed to a stipendiary curacy shall, before obtaining such licence, present to the bishop of the diocese the form of nomination of a curate signed by the minister having the cure of souls in the place wherein he is to serve, and the Stipendiary Curate's Declaration, signed by himself and the said minister, such declaration being in the form following:

   I, A.B., incumbent of   *, in the county of*   *,* bona fide *undertake to pay C.D., of*   *, in the county of*   *, the annual sum of*   *pounds as a stipend for his services as curate; and I, C.D.,* bona fide *intend to receive the whole of the said stipend. And each of us, the said A.B. and C.D., declare that no abatement is to be made out of the said stipend in respect of rent or consideration for the use of the glebe house; and that I, A.B., undertake to pay the same, and I, C.D., intend to receive the same, without any deduction or abatement whatever, except in respect of contributions under the Clergy Pensions Measure, 1961.*

4   No stipendiary curate shall be licensed to serve in more than one church or chapel, except they be churches of one united benefice, or held in plurality, or the chapel be dependent on the parish church.

5   Any bishop may revoke summarily, and without further process, any licence granted to any minister within his diocese, for any cause which shall appear to him to be good and reasonable, after having given such minister sufficient opportunity of showing reason to the contrary: Provided that any such minister may, within one month after service upon him of such revocation, appeal to the archbishop of the province, who shall confirm or annul such revocation as to him shall appear just and proper and from whose decision therein there shall be no appeal. During a vacancy of the see, the powers of a bishop under this paragraph shall be exercisable by the archbishop of the province in which the diocese is situate, and the proviso shall not apply.

C 13   Of the Oath of Allegiance

1   Every person whose election to any archbishopric or bishopric is to be confirmed, or who is to be consecrated or translated to any suffragan bishopric, or to be ordained priest or deacon, or to be instituted to any benefice, or to be licensed to any perpetual curacy, lectureship, or preachership, shall first, in the presence of the archbishop or bishop by whom his election to such arch- bishopric or bishopric is to be confirmed, or in whose province

such suffragan bishopric is situate, or by whom he is to be ordained, instituted, or licensed, or of the commissary of such archbishop or bishop, take and subscribe the Oath of Allegiance in the form following: *I, A.B., do swear that I will be faithful and bear true allegiance to Her Majesty Queen Elizabeth II, her heirs and successors, according to law: So help me God.*

2 The aforesaid Oath of Allegiance shall not be required to be taken (*a*) by any subject or citizen of a foreign state whom either archbishop, calling to assist him such bishops as he thinks fit, shall consecrate to officiate as a bishop in any foreign state, or (*b*) by any overseas clergyman to whom section 2 of the Overseas and Other Clergy (Ministry and Ordination) Measure, 1967, applies or any other person ordained under section 5 of that Measure for ministry overseas, if the bishop dispenses with the said oath.

C 14 Of the Oaths of Obedience

1 Every person whose election to any bishopric is to be confirmed, or who is to be consecrated bishop or translated to any suffragan bishopric, shall first take the oath of due obedience to the archbishop and to the metropolitical Church of the province wherein he is to exercise the episcopal office in the form and manner prescribed in and by the Ordinal.

2 Either archbishop consecrating any person to exercise episcopal functions elsewhere than in England may dispense with the said oath.

3 Every person who is to be ordained priest or deacon, or to be instituted to any benefice, or to be licensed either to any perpetual curacy, lectureship, preachership, or stipendiary curacy, or to serve in any place, shall first take the Oath of Canonical Obedience to the bishop of the diocese by whom he is to be ordained, instituted, or licensed, in the presence of the said bishop or his commissary, and in the form following:

I, A.B., do swear by Almighty God that I will pay true and canonical obedience to the Lord Bishop of C. and his successors in all things lawful and honest: So help me God.

C 15   Of the Declaration of Assent

1 (1) *a* Every person whose election to any archbishopric or
          bishopric is to be confirmed or who is to be consecrated
          bishop or appointed to any suffragan bishopric shall
          first in the presence of the archbishop or bishop by
          whom his election is to be confirmed or in whose
          province or diocese such suffragan bishopric is situate
          make and subscribe the Declaration of Assent in the
          manner and form set out below.

      b Every person who is to be ordained priest or deacon
          shall before ordination make and subscribe the said
          declaration in the presence of the archbishop or bishop
          by whom he is to be ordained.

      c Every person who is to be instituted or admitted to any
          benefice or other ecclesiastical preferment or licensed
          to any perpetual curacy, lectureship, or preachership
          shall first make and subscribe the said declaration in
          the presence of the bishop by whom he is to be insti-
          tuted or licensed or of the bishop's commissary.

      d Every person who is to be licensed to any curacy shall
          first make and subscribe the said declaration in the
          presence of the bishop by whom he is to be licensed or
          his commissary unless he shall have been ordained the
          same day and has already made the said declaration.

   (2) For the avoiding of all ambiguity every person required to
        make and subscribe the said declaration shall make and
        subscribe in this order and form of words, setting down
        both his Christian names and surname, viz.:

*I, A.B., do solemnly make the following declaration: I assent to
the Thirty-nine Articles of Religion, and to the Book of Common
Prayer and of the Ordering of Bishops, Priests, and Deacons. I
believe the doctrine of the Church of England as therein set forth to
be agreeable to the Word of God; and in public prayer and administration of the sacraments I will use the form in the said book
prescribed and none other, except so far as shall be ordered by lawful
authority.*

2   Every minister instituted or collated to a benefice with a cure
of souls or licensed to a perpetual curacy shall, on the first Lord's
Day or on such other Lord's Day as the Ordinary may appoint
and allow on which he officiates in the church of the benefice or
perpetual curacy or, if the benefice or perpetual curacy is a united
benefice comprising more than one parish and the parishes have

not been united, in the parish church of one of the parishes, publicly and openly, in the presence of the congregation there assembled, read the Thirty-nine Articles of Religion, and immediately after reading the same shall make the Declaration of Assent, adding after the words "Articles of Religion" in the said declaration the words "which I have now read before you".

3 Every minister licensed to a stipendiary curacy shall, on the first Lord's Day on which he officiates in the church or in one of the churches in which he is licensed to serve, publicly and openly make the Declaration of Assent, in the presence of the congregation here assembled, and at the time of divine service.

4 Any person who in pursuance of a request and commission from a bishop of any diocese in England has been ordained by an overseas bishop within the meaning of the Overseas and Other Clergy (Ministry and Ordination) Measure, 1967, or a bishop in a Church not in communion with the Church of England, whose orders are recognized or accepted by the Church of England, shall be deemed to be ordained by a bishop of a diocese in England and accordingly shall make the Declaration of Assent in the form set out in paragraph 1 of this Canon.

C 16 Of the Declaration against Simony

1 Every person whose election to any archbishopric or bishopric is to be confirmed, or who is to be consecrated bishop or translated to any suffragan bishopric, or is to be instituted to any deanery, archdeaconry, or canonry, shall first in the presence of the archbishop or bishop by whom his election to such archbishopric or bishopric is to be confirmed, or in whose province such suffragan bishopric is situate, or by whom he is to be instituted, or of the commissary of such archbishop or bishop, make and subscribe this declaration in the manner and form following, the same to be made by everyone whom it concerns in his own person, and not by a proctor:

I, A.B., solemnly declare that I have not made, by myself or by any other person on my behalf, any payment, contract, or promise of any kind whatsoever which to the best of my knowledge or belief is simoniacal, touching or concerning the preferment of   ; nor will I at any time hereafter perform or satisfy, in whole or in part, any such kind of payment, contract, or promise made by any other without my knowledge or consent.

2   Every person who is to be instituted to any benefice with cure
of souls, or to be licensed to any perpetual curacy, shall first, in
the presence of the bishop by whom he is to be instituted or
licensed, or of the commissary of such bishop, make and subscribe
this declaration in the manner and form following, the same to be
made by everyone whom it concerns in his own person, and not by
a proctor:

*I, A.B., hereby solemnly and sincerely declare in reference to the
presentation made to me of the   of
in the county of   and diocese of   as
follows:*

*(i)   I have not received the presentation of the said
in consideration of any sum of money, reward, gift, profit, or benefit
directly or indirectly given or promised by me, or by any person to
my knowledge or with my consent, to any person whatsoever, and I
will not at any time hereafter perform or satisfy any payment, contract, or promise made in respect of that presentation by any person
without my knowledge or consent.*

*(ii)   I have not entered, nor, to the best of my knowledge or belief,
has any person entered into any bond, covenant, or other assurance
or engagement, that I should at any time resign the said*

*(iii)   I have not by myself, nor to my knowledge has any person on
my behalf, for any sum of money, reward, gift, profit, or advantage,
or for or by means of any promise, agreement (not being an agreement lawfully made for exchange of benefices), grant, bond, covenant,
or other assurance of or for any sum of money, reward, gift, profit,
or benefit whatsoever, directly or indirectly, procured the now existing
avoidance of the said*

*(iv)   I have not, with respect of the said presentation, been party
or privy to any agreement which is invalid under section one, sub-
section three, of the Benefices Act, 1898.*

Dated this   day of   19

C 17   Of archbishops

1   By virtue of their respective offices, the Archbishop of Canterbury is styled Primate of All England and Metropolitan, and the
Archbishop of York Primate of England and Metropolitan.

2   The archbishop has throughout his province at all times
metropolitical jurisdiction, as superintendent of all ecclesiastical
matters therein, to correct and supply the defects of other bishops,
and, during the time of his metropolitical visitation, jurisdiction

as Ordinary, except in places and over persons exempt by law or custom.

3   Such jurisdiction is exercised by the archbishop himself, or by a vicar-general, official, or other commissary to whom authority in that behalf shall have been formally committed by the archbishop concerned.

4   The archbishop is, within his province, the principal minister, and to him belongs the right of confirming the election of every person to a bishopric, of being the chief consecrator at the consecration of every bishop, of receiving such appeals in his provincial court as may be provided by law, of holding metropolitical visitations at times or places limited by law or custom, and of presiding in the Convocation of the province either in person or by such deputy as he may lawfully appoint. In the province of Canterbury, the Bishop of London or, in his absence, the Bishop of Winchester, has the right to be so appointed; and in their absence the archbishop shall appoint some other diocesan bishop of the province.

5   By ancient custom, no Act or Canon is held to be an Act or Canon of the Convocation of the province unless it shall have received the assent of the archbishop.

6   By statute law it belongs to the archbishop to give permission to officiate within his province to any minister who has been ordained priest or deacon by an overseas bishop within the meaning of the Overseas and Other Clergy (Ministry and Ordination) Measure, 1967, or a bishop in a Church not in communion with the Church of England whose orders are recognized or accepted by the Church of England, and thereupon such minister shall possess all such rights and advantages and be subject to all such duties and liabilities as he would have possessed and been subject to if he had been ordained by the bishop of a diocese in the province of Canterbury or York.

7   By the laws of this realm the Archbishop of Canterbury is empowered to grant such licences or dispensations as are therein set forth and provided, and such licences or dispensations, being confirmed by the authority of the Queen's Majesty, have force and authority not only within the province of Canterbury but throughout all England.

C 18   Of diocesan bishops

1   Every bishop is the chief pastor of all that are within his diocese, as well laity as clergy, and their father in God; it appertains to his office to teach and to uphold sound and wholesome doctrine, and to banish and drive away all erroneous and strange opinions; and, himself an example of righteous and godly living, it is his duty to set forward and maintain quietness, love, and peace among all men.

2   Every bishop has within his diocese jurisdiction as Ordinary, except in places and over persons exempt by law or custom.

3   Such jurisdiction is exercised by the bishop himself, or by a vicar-general, official, or other commissary, to whom authority in that behalf shall have been formally committed by the bishop concerned.

4   Every bishop is, within his diocese, the principal minister, and to him belongs the right, save in places and over persons exempt by law or custom, of celebrating the rites of ordination and confirmation; of conducting, ordering, controlling, and authorizing all services in churches, chapels, churchyards, and consecrated burial grounds; of granting a faculty or licence for all alterations, additions, removals, or repairs to the walls, fabric, ornaments, or furniture of the same; of consecrating new churches, churchyards, and burial grounds; of instituting to all vacant benefices, whether of his own collation or of the presentation of others; of admitting by licence to all other vacant ecclesiastical offices; of holding visitations at times limited by law or custom to the end that he may get some good knowledge of the state, sufficiency, and ability of the clergy and other persons whom he is to visit; of summoning all synods and diocesan conferences; and of presiding therein, either in person or by such deputy as he may lawfully appoint.

5   No resolution in any such synod or diocesan conference shall have effect without the sanction of the bishop, which is not lightly nor without grave cause to be withheld.

6   Every bishop shall be faithful in admitting persons into holy orders and in celebrating the rite of confirmation as often and in as many places as shall be convenient, and shall provide, as much as in him lies, that in every place within his diocese there shall be sufficient priests to minister the word and sacraments to the people that are therein.

7   Every bishop shall correct and punish all such as be unquiet, disobedient, or criminous, within his diocese, according to such authority as he has by God's Word and is committed to him by the laws and ordinances of this realm.

8   Every bishop shall reside within his diocese, saving the ancient right of any bishop, when resident in any house in London during his attendance on the Parliament, or on the Court, or for the purpose of performing any other duties of his office, to be taken and accounted as resident within his own diocese.

C 19   Of guardians of spiritualities

1   Whenever the archiepiscopal see be vacant the guardianship of the spiritualities belongs, according to the custom of the Church of England from ancient times, to the dean and chapter of the metropolitical church of the province, who shall exercise the spiritual jurisdiction of the province and diocese during the vacancy.

2   Whenever a bishopric be vacant the guardianship of the spiritualities belongs to the dean and chapter of the cathedral church of the diocese, unless by prescription or composition it belongs to the archbishop of the province acting by and through such person or persons as he may nominate according to the prescription or composition.

3   The guardian or guardians of the spiritualities shall exercise the spiritual jurisdiction of the diocese during the vacancy, including the giving of institution to benefices, the granting of licences for the solemnization of matrimony without the publication of banns, the granting of commissions for ordination *sede vacante*: Provided that their powers shall not extend to such matters as are excluded from their jurisdiction by the laws of the realm, or to the presentation to benefices *sede vacante* of which the archbishop or bishop is patron; which presentation belongs to the Crown by royal prerogative.

C 20   Of bishops suffragan

1   Every bishop suffragan shall endeavour himself faithfully to execute such things pertaining to the episcopal office as shall be commissioned to him by the bishop of the diocese to whom he shall be suffragan.

2   Every bishop suffragan shall use, have, or execute only such jurisdiction or episcopal power or authority in any diocese as shall be licensed or limited to him to use, have, or execute by the bishop of the same.

3   Every bishop suffragan shall reside within the diocese of the bishop to whom he shall be suffragan, except he have a licence from that bishop to reside elsewhere.

C 21   Of deans or provosts, and canons residentiary of cathedral or collegiate churches

1   No person shall be capable of receiving the appointment of dean, provost, or canon until he has been six years complete in priest's orders, except in the case of a canonry annexed to any professorship, headship, or other office in any university.

2   The dean, or provost, of every cathedral or collegiate church, and the canons residentiary of the same, shall take care that the statutes and laudable customs of their church (not being contrary to the Word of God or prerogative royal), the statutes of this realm concerning ecclesiastical order, and all other constitutions set forth and confirmed by Her Majesty's authority, and such as shall be enjoined by the bishop of the diocese in his visitation, according to the statutes and customs of the same church, and the ecclesiastical laws of the realm, shall be diligently observed.

3   The dean, or provost, and the canons residentiary shall be resident in their cathedral or collegiate church for the time prescribed by law and by the statutes of the said cathedral or collegiate church, and shall there preach the Word of God and perform all the duties of their office, except they shall be otherwise hindered by weighty and urgent causes.

4   The dean, or provost, and the canons residentiary of every cathedral or collegiate church, together with the minor canons, vicars choral, and other ministers of the same, shall provide, as far as in them lies, that during the time of divine service in the said church all things be done with such reverence, care, and solemnity as shall set forth the honour and glory of Almighty God.

C 22   Of archdeacons

1   No person shall be capable of receiving the appointment of archdeacon until he has been six years complete in priest's orders.

2   Every archdeacon within his archdeaconry exercises the jurisdiction which he has therein as an ordinary jurisdiction.

3   Such jurisdiction is exercised either by the archdeacon in person or by an official or commissary to whom authority in that behalf shall have been formally committed by the archdeacon concerned.

4   Every archdeacon shall within his archdeaconry carry out his duties under the bishop and shall assist the bishop in his pastoral care and office, and particularly he shall see that all such as hold any ecclesiastical office within the same perform their duties with diligence, and shall bring to the bishop's attention what calls for correction or merits praise.

5   Every archdeacon shall within his archdeaconry hold yearly visitations save when inhibited by a superior Ordinary; he shall also survey in person or by deputy all churches, chancels, and church-yards and give direction for the amendment of all defects in the walls, fabric, ornaments, and furniture of the same, and in parti-cular shall exercise the powers conferred on him by the Inspection of Churches Measure, 1954; he shall also, on receiving Letters Mandatory of the bishop, induct any priest who has been insti-tuted to a benefice into possession of the temporalities of the same.

C 23   Of rural deans

1   Every rural dean shall report to the bishop any matter in any parish within the deanery which it may be necessary or useful for the bishop to know, particularly any case of serious illness or other form of distress amongst the clergy, the vacancy of any cure of souls and the measures taken by the sequestrators to secure the ministration of the word and sacraments and other rites of the Church during the said vacancy, and any case of a minister from another diocese officiating in any place otherwise than as provided in Canon C 8.

2   In the case of any omission in any parish to prepare and main-tain a church electoral roll or to form or maintain a parochial church council or to hold the annual parochial church meeting,

the rural dean on such omission being brought to his notice shall ascertain and report to the bishop the cause thereof.

3   If at any time the rural dean has reason to believe that there is any serious defect in the fabric, ornaments, and furniture of any church or chapel, or that the buildings of any benefice are in a state of disrepair, he shall report the matter to the archdeacon.

4   Every rural dean shall summon and preside over the ruri-decanal chapter at least twice a year, and the ruridecanal conference, if any, as occasion may require.

C 24   Of priests having a cure of souls

1   Every priest having a cure of souls shall provide that, in the absence of reasonable hindrance, Morning and Evening Prayer daily and on appointed days the Litany shall be said in the church, or one of the churches, of which he is the minister.

2   Every priest having a cure of souls shall, except for some reasonable cause approved by the bishop of the diocese, celebrate, or cause to be celebrated, the Holy Communion on all Sundays and other greater Feast Days and on Ash Wednesday, and shall administer the sacraments and other rites prescribed in and by the Book of Common Prayer, diligently, as occasion may require.

3   Every priest having a cure of souls shall, except for some reasonable cause approved by the bishop of the diocese, preach, or cause to be preached, a sermon in his church at least once each Sunday.

4   He shall instruct the children, or cause them to be instructed, in the Christian faith; and shall use such opportunities of teaching or visiting in the schools within his cure as are open to him.

5   He shall carefully prepare, or cause to be prepared, all such as desire to be confirmed and, if satisfied of their fitness, shall present them to the bishop for confirmation.

6   He shall be diligent in visiting his parishioners, particularly those who are sick and infirm; and he shall provide opportunities whereby any of his parishioners may resort unto him for spiritual counsel and advice.

7 He shall seek the co-operation of the parochial church council in the initiation, conduct, and development of the worship and work of the Church.

8 If at any time he shall be unable to discharge his duties whether from non-residence or some other cause, he shall provide for his cure to be supplied by a priest licensed or otherwise approved by the bishop of the diocese.

C 25   Of the residence of priests on their benefices

1 Every beneficed priest shall keep residence on his benefice, or on one of them if he shall hold two or more in plurality, and in the house of residence (if any) belonging thereto.

2 No beneficed priest shall be absent from his benefice, or from the house of residence belonging thereto, for a period exceeding the space of three months together, or to be accounted at several times in any one year, except he have a licence to be so absent, granted by the bishop of the diocese subject to the statutory provisions in this behalf for the time being in force, or be otherwise legally exempt from residence.

3 Any beneficed priest, within one month after refusal of any such licence, may appeal to the archbishop of the province, who shall confirm such refusal or direct the bishop to grant a licence, as shall seem to the said archbishop just and proper.

4 In the case of any benefice in which there is no house, or no fit house of residence, the priest holding that benefice may be licensed by the bishop of the diocese to reside in some fit and convenient house, although not belonging to that benefice: Provided that such house be within three miles of the church or chapel of the benefice, or, if the same be in any city or borough town or market town, within two miles of such church or chapel.

C 26   Of the manner of life of ministers

1 Every bishop, priest, and deacon is under obligation, not being let by sickness or some other urgent cause, to say daily the Morning and Evening Prayer, either privately or openly; and to celebrate the Holy Communion, or be present thereat, on all Sundays and other principal Feast Days. He is also to be diligent in daily prayer and intercession, in examination of his conscience,

and in the study of the holy Scriptures and such other studies as pertain to his ministerial duties.

2   A minister shall not give himself to such occupations, habits, or recreations as do not befit his sacred calling, or may be detrimental to the performance of the duties of his office, or tend to be a just cause of offence to others; and at all times he shall be diligent to frame and fashion his life and that of his family according to the doctrine of Christ, and to make himself and them, as much as in him lies, wholesome examples and patterns to the flock of Christ.

C 27   Of the dress of ministers

The apparel of a bishop, priest, or deacon shall be suitable to his office; and, save for purposes of recreation and other justifiable reasons, shall be such as to be a sign and mark of his holy calling and ministry as well to others as to those committed to his spiritual charge.

C 28   Of the occupations of ministers

1   No minister holding ecclesiastical office shall engage in trade or any other occupation in such manner as to affect the performance of the duties of his office, except so far as he be authorized so to do under the statutory provisions in this behalf for the time being in force or he have a licence so to do granted by the bishop of the diocese.

2   The bishop of the diocese shall have power to grant such a licence after consultation with the parochial church council of the parish in which the minister holds office or to refuse such a licence after consultation with that council and also with the ministerial committee of the diocese constituted under the provisions of the Incumbents (Disability) Measure, 1945.

3   If the bishop of the diocese shall refuse such a licence, the minister may within one month of such refusal appeal to the archbishop of the province, who shall confirm or overrule such refusal as may seem good to him.

4   During a vacancy of the see, the powers of the bishop of a diocese under paragraphs 1 and 2 of this Canon shall be exercisable by the archbishop of the province in which the diocese is situate, and paragraph 3 of this Canon shall not apply.

Section D

THE ORDER OF DEACONESSES

D 1 Of the order of deaconesses

1 The order of deaconesses is the one order of ministry in the Church of England to which women are admitted by prayer and the laying on of hands by the bishop.

2 It belongs to the office of a deaconess, in the place where she is licensed to serve, to exercise a pastoral care especially over women, young people, and children, to visit the sick and the whole, to instruct the people in the faith, and to prepare them for the reception of the sacraments.

3 The bishop may permit a deaconess in any church or chapel within his jurisdiction at the invitation of the minister thereof:

a To read in case of need the services of Morning and Evening Prayer and the Litany, except those portions reserved to the priest, and to lead in prayer.

b To instruct and preach except during the service of Holy Communion.

4 The order of deaconesses is not one of the holy orders of the Church of England, and accordingly deaconesses may accept membership of any lay assembly of the Church of England without prejudice to the standing of their order.

D 2 Of admission to the order of deaconesses

1 Every woman to be admitted to the order of deaconesses shall be at least twenty-five years of age, baptized, confirmed, and shall satisfy the bishop that she is a regular communicant of the Church of England.

2 Every woman who is to be admitted to the order of deaconesses shall first present to the bishop of the diocese:

a a certificate signed by a person approved by the bishop that she has been nominated to exercise the office of deaconess within his diocese either in a cure of souls or in a wider area, or is a teacher or lecturer in a school or college or is living under vows in the house of a religious order or community; the said school, college, or house of a religious order or community being situated within such diocese;

b (i) her birth certificate;

(ii) a certificate or other evidence of her baptism and confirmation;

(iii) testimonials of her good life, of her conformity to the doctrine, discipline, and worship of the Church of England, and of her general fitness for the office of a deaconess, from two beneficed priests, a deaconess holding a bishop's licence, and the head of the house, hostel, or college wherein she shall have been trained for the said office;

(iv) a certificate signed by the officiating minister and one churchwarden of the parish or ecclesiastical district wherein she usually resides or in which her name is on the electoral roll, that notice in a form approved by the Ordinary was given in the church of the same in the time of divine service on some Sunday at least a month before the day appointed for her admission to the order of deaconesses, of her intention of offering herself as a candidate for the said order, and that no cause or impediment why she should not be admitted to the same was alleged by any person present.

3   No woman shall be admitted to the order of deaconesses except she be found on examination, held by the bishop or by competent persons appointed by him for this purpose, to possess a sufficient knowledge of holy Scripture and of the doctrine, discipline, and worship of the Church of England.

4   No woman shall be admitted to the order of deaconesses who is suffering or who has suffered from any physical or mental infirmity which, in the opinion of the bishop, will prevent her from exercising the office of a deaconess.

5   Every woman who is to be admitted to the order of deaconesses shall, in the presence of the bishop by whom she is to be so admitted or of the commissary of such bishop, make and subscribe the Declaration following: *I, A.B., assent to the Thirty-nine Articles of Religion and to the Book of Common Prayer, and I believe the doctrines of the Church of England, as therein set forth, to be agreeable to the Word of God*; and take the oath following: *I, A.B., will give due obedience to the Lord Bishop of C. and his successors, in all things lawful and honest: So help me God.*

6   A woman shall be admitted to the order of deaconesses according to the form of service sanctioned by lawful authority.

D 3   Of the licensing of deaconesses

1   No deaconess shall exercise her office in any diocese until she has been licensed so to do by the bishop thereof: Provided that, when any deaconess is to exercise her office temporarily in any diocese, the written permission of the bishop shall suffice.

2   Every deaconess who is to be licensed to exercise her office in any place shall make and subscribe a declaration and take an oath in the form and manner prescribed for a deaconess before her admission to the order.

3   Every bishop, before licensing a deaconess to exercise her office in any place, shall satisfy himself that adequate provision has been made for her salary, for her insurance against sickness or accident, and for a pension on her retirement.

4   The bishop of every diocese shall keep a register book wherein shall be entered the names of every person whom he has either admitted to the order of deaconesses or licensed to exercise the office of a deaconess in his diocese.

THE LAY OFFICERS OF THE CHURCH OF ENGLAND

Section II.

THE LAY OFFICERS OF THE
CHURCH OF ENGLAND

E 1   Of churchwardens

1   The churchwardens of parishes and districts shall be chosen in accordance with the Churchwardens (Appointment and Resignation) Measure, 1964, and any other Measure, Act, or scheme affecting churchwardens.

2   At a time and place to be appointed by the Ordinary, as soon as may be after the week following Easter Week, each person chosen for the office of churchwarden shall appear before the Ordinary, or his substitute duly appointed, and be admitted to the office of churchwarden after subscribing the declaration that he will faithfully and diligently perform the duties of his office, and making the same in the presence of the Ordinary or his substitute.

3   Subject to any provision of any Measure, Act, or scheme relating to the resignation or vacation of their office, the churchwardens so chosen and admitted shall continue in their office until they, or others as their successors, be admitted in like manner by the Ordinary.

4   The churchwardens when admitted are officers of the Ordinary. They shall discharge such duties as are by law and custom assigned to them; they shall be foremost in representing the laity and in co-operating with the incumbent; they shall use their best endeavours by example and precept to encourage the parishioners in the practice of true religion and to promote unity and peace among them. They shall also maintain order and decency in the church and churchyard, especially during the time of divine service.

5   In the churchwardens is vested the property in the plate, ornaments, and other movable goods of the church, and they shall keep an inventory thereof which they shall revise from time to time as occasion may require. On going out of office they shall duly deliver to their successors any goods of the church remaining in their hands together with the said inventory, which shall be checked by their successors.

E 2   Of sidesmen or assistants to the churchwardens

1   The sidesmen of the parish are by law elected by the annual parochial church meeting and the minister, provided that, if the annual meeting and the minister are unable to agree, one half of the sidesmen are elected by the annual meeting and one half are appointed by the minister.

2   No person whose name is not on the church electoral roll is eligible as a sidesman, but all persons whose names are on the roll are so eligible.

3   It shall be the duty of the sidesmen to promote the cause of true religion in the parish and to assist the churchwardens in the discharge of their duties in maintaining order and decency in the church and churchyard, especially during the time of divine service.

E 3   Of parish clerks and other officers

In any parish in which the services of a parish clerk, sexton, verger, or other officer are required the minister and the parochial church council may in accordance with the law appoint some fit and proper person to these offices to perform such services upon such terms and conditions as they may think fit.

E 4   Of readers

1   A lay person, whether man or woman, who is baptized and confirmed and who satisfies the bishop that he is a regular communicant of the Church of England may be admitted by the bishop of the diocese to the office of reader in the Church and licensed by him to perform any duty or duties which may lawfully be performed by a reader according to the provisions of paragraph 2 of this Canon or which may from time to time be so determined by Act of Convocation.

2   It shall be lawful for a reader:

a   to visit the sick, to read and pray with them, to teach in Sunday school and elsewhere, and generally to undertake such pastoral and educational work and to give such assistance to any minister as the bishop may direct;

b   during the time of divine service to read Morning and Evening Prayer (save for the Absolution), to publish banns of marriage at Morning or Evening Prayer (on occasions on which a layman is permitted by the statute law so to do, and in accordance with the requirements of that law), to read the Word of God, to preach, to catechize the children, and to receive and present the offerings of the people; and give such further assistance as may be authorized under Canon B 12.

3   The bishop of every diocese shall keep a register book wherein shall be entered the names of every person whom he has either admitted to the office of reader or licensed to exercise that office in any place.

E 5   Of the nomination and admission of readers

1   A candidate for the office of reader in a parish or district shall be nominated to the bishop by the minister of that parish or district; and a candidate for the said office in a wider area by one of the rural deans or archdeacons after consultation with the minister of his parish or district.

2   The nominator in making such nomination shall also satisfy the bishop that the said person is of good life, sound in faith, a regular communicant, and well fitted for the work of a reader, and provide all such other information about the said person and the duties which it is desired that he should perform as the bishop may require.

3   No person shall be admitted to the office of reader in the Church except it be found on examination, held by the bishop or by competent persons appointed by the bishop for this purpose, that he possesses a sufficient knowledge of holy Scripture and of the doctrine and worship of the Church of England as set forth in the Book of Common Prayer, that he is able to read the services of the Church plainly, distinctly, audibly, and reverently, and that he is capable both of teaching and preaching.

4   Every person to be admitted to the office of reader shall first in the presence of the bishop by whom he is to be so admitted, or of the commissary of such bishop, make and sign the declarations following:

I, A.B., about to be admitted to the office of a reader in the Church, do hereby declare as follows: I have been baptized and confirmed, and I am a regular communicant of the Church of England. I assent to the Thirty-nine Articles of Religion and to the Book of Common Prayer, and I believe the doctrine of the Church of England, as therein set forth, to be agreeable to the Word of God. I will give due obedience to the Bishop of C. and his successors in all things lawful and honest.

5   The bishop shall admit a person to the office of reader by the delivery of the New Testament, but without imposition of hands.

6   The bishop shall give to the newly admitted reader a certificate of his admission to the office; and the admission shall not be repeated if the reader shall move to another diocese.

E 6   Of the licensing of readers

1   No person who has been admitted to the office of reader shall exercise his office in any diocese until he has been licensed so to do by the bishop thereof: Provided that, when any reader is to exercise his office temporarily in any diocese, the written permission of the bishop shall suffice.

2   Every reader who is to be licensed to exercise his office in any diocese shall first, in the presence of the bishop by whom he is to be so licensed, or of the commissary of such bishop, (*a*) make the declarations of assent and of obedience in the form and manner prescribed by paragraph 4 of Canon E 5; (*b*) make and subscribe the declaration following:

I, A.B., about to be licensed to exercise the office of reader in the parish (or diocese) of C., do hereby promise to endeavour, as far as in me lies, to promote peace and unity, and to conduct myself as becomes a worker for Christ, for the good of his Church, and for the spiritual welfare of my fellow men. I will give due obedience to the Bishop of C. and his successors and the minister in whose cure I may serve, in all things lawful and honest.

3   A reader, when required to do so by the bishop, shall cease from the exercise of his functions and return his licence to the bishop for cancellation.

4   No bishop shall license any reader to be a stipendiary in any place until he has satisfied himself that adequate provision has been made for the stipend of the said reader, for his insurance against sickness or accident, and for a pension on his retirement.

E 7   Of the commissioning and licensing
of women workers

1   A woman who satisfies the bishop of the diocese that she is baptized, confirmed, and a regular communicant of the Church of England, and possesses the necessary qualifications, may be commissioned by him as a woman worker of the Church.

2   The bishop shall give to every woman so commissioned by him a certificate of her commission as a woman worker of the Church, and the commission shall not be repeated if she shall move to another diocese.

3   No woman who has been commissioned as a woman worker of the Church shall serve as such in any diocese except she shall have, in addition to the certificate of her commission, a licence so to do from the bishop thereof: Provided that, when any woman worker is to serve temporarily in any diocese, the written permission of the bishop shall suffice.

4   No bishop shall commission or license any woman as a woman worker, except he be satisfied that

a   she is competent to carry out the duties which may be assigned to her;
b   if she is to be a stipendiary worker in any place, adequate provision has been made for her salary, for her insurance against sickness or accident, and for a pension on her retirement.

5   Every woman who is to be commissioned or licensed as a woman worker shall, in the presence of the bishop by whom she is to be so commissioned or licensed, or of the commissary of such bishop, make and subscribe the declarations following:

a   *I, A.B., assent to the Book of Common Prayer, and I believe the doctrine of the Church of England, as therein set forth, to be agreeable to the Word of God;* and
b   *I, A.B., will give due obedience to the bishop and his successors in all things lawful and honest.*

6   The bishop of every diocese shall keep a register book wherein shall be entered the name of every person either commissioned or licensed by him as a woman worker, together with the particular duties which such person has been licensed to perform.

Section F

THINGS APPERTAINING TO CHURCHES

F 1   Of the font

1   In every church and chapel where baptism is to be administered, there shall be provided a decent font with a cover for the keeping clean thereof.

2   The font shall stand as near to the principal entrance as conveniently may be, except there be a custom to the contrary or the Ordinary otherwise direct; and shall be set in as spacious and well-ordered surroundings as possible.

3   The font bowl shall only be used for the water at the administration of Holy Baptism and for no other purpose whatsoever.

F 2   Of the holy table

1   In every church and chapel a convenient and decent table, of wood, stone, or other suitable material, shall be provided for the celebration of the Holy Communion, and shall stand in the main body of the church or in the chancel where Morning and Evening Prayer are appointed to be said. Any dispute as to the position where the table shall stand shall be determined by the Ordinary.

2   The table, as becomes the table of the Lord, shall be kept in a sufficient and seemly manner, and from time to time repaired, and shall be covered in the time of divine service with a covering of silk or other decent stuff, and with a fair white linen cloth at the time of the celebration of the Holy Communion.

F 3   Of the communion plate

1   In every church and chapel there shall be provided, for the celebration of the Holy Communion, a chalice for the wine and a paten or other vessel for the bread, of gold, silver, or other suitable metal. There shall also be provided a bason for the reception of the alms and other devotions of the people, and a convenient cruet or flagon for bringing the wine to the communion table.

2   It is the duty of the minister of every church or chapel to see that the communion plate is kept washed and clean, and ready for the celebration of the Holy Communion.

F 4   Of the communion linen

In every parochial church and chapel there shall be provided and
maintained a sufficient number of fair white linen cloths for the
covering of the communion table and of other fair linen cloths for
the use of the priest during the celebration of Holy Communion.

F 5   Of surplices for the minister

In every church and chapel surplices shall be provided and maintained in a clean condition for the use of the minister.

F 6   Of the reading desks and pulpit

In every church and chapel there shall be provided convenient
desks for the reading of Prayers and God's Word, and, unless it
be not required, a decent pulpit for the sermon, to be set in a
convenient place; which place, in the case of any dispute, shall be
determined by the Ordinary.

F 7   Of seats in church

1   In every church and chapel there shall be provided seats for the
use of the parishioners and others who attend divine service.

2   In parish churches and chapels it belongs to the churchwardens, acting for this purpose as the officers of the Ordinary and
subject to his direction, to allocate the seats amongst the
parishioners and others in such manner as the service of God may
be best celebrated in the church or chapel; saving the right of the
minister to allocate seats in the chancel and the rights of any
person to a seat or to allocate seats conferred by faculty, prescription, or statutory authority.

3   Such allocation of seats to non-parishioners shall not interfere
with the rights of the parishioners to have seats in the main body
of the church.

F 8   Of church bells

1   In every church and chapel there shall be provided at least one
bell to ring the people to divine service.

2   No bell in any church or chapel shall be rung contrary to the
direction of the minister.

F 9   Of the Bible and the Book of Common Prayer for the use of the minister

In every church and chapel there shall be provided for the use of the minister a Bible, including the Apocrypha, and a Book of Common Prayer, both of large size; a convenient Bible to be kept in the pulpit for the use of the preacher; and a service book, together with a cushion or desk, for use at the communion table.

F 10   Of the alms box

In every parochial church and chapel there shall be provided in a convenient place a box for the alms of the people; which alms are to be applied to such uses as the minister and parochial church council shall think fit; wherein if they disagree, the Ordinary shall determine the disposal thereof.

F 11   Of the register books and their custody

1   In every parish church and chapel where baptism is to be administered or matrimony solemnized there shall be provided register books of baptism, banns and marriage respectively, and, if a churchyard or burial ground belonging to such church or chapel is used for burials, a register book of burials.

2   Register books shall be provided, maintained, and kept in accordance with the Statutes and Measures relating thereto, and the rules and regulations made thereunder and from time to time in force.

3   In every parish church and chapel there shall also be provided a register book of confirmations.

F 12   Of the register book of services

1   A register book of services shall be provided in all churches and chapels.

2   In the said register book shall be recorded every service of public worship, together with the name of the officiating minister and of the preacher (if he be other than the officiating minister), the number of communicants, and the amount of any alms or other collections and, if desired, notes of significant events.

F 13   Of the care and repair of churches

1   The churches and chapels in every parish shall be decently kept
and from time to time, as occasion may require, shall be well and
sufficiently repaired and all things therein shall be maintained in
such an orderly and decent fashion as best becomes the House of
God.

2   The like care shall be taken that the churchyards be duly
fenced, and that the said fences be maintained at the charge of
those to whom by law or custom the liability belongs, and that the
churchyards be kept in such an orderly and decent manner as
becomes consecrated ground.

3   It shall be the duty of the minister and churchwardens, if any
alterations, additions, removals, or repairs are proposed to be
made in the fabric, ornaments, or furniture of the church, to
obtain the faculty or licence of the Ordinary before proceeding
to execute the same: Save that in repairs to a church not involving
any substantial alteration, or in the redecoration of a church, a
certificate issued with the approval of the diocesan advisory
committee for the care of churches by the archdeacon of the archdeaconry in which such church is situated shall suffice.

4   In the case of every parochial church and chapel, a record of
all alterations, additions, removals, or repairs so executed shall be
kept in a book to be provided for the purpose and the record shall
indicate where specifications and plans may be inspected if not
deposited with the book.

F 14   Of the provision of things appertaining to churches

The things appertaining to churches and chapels, and the obligations relating thereto, and to the care and repair of churches,
chapels, and churchyards referred to in the foregoing Canons shall,
in so far as the law may from time to time require, be provided
and performed in the case of parochial churches and chapels by
and at the charge of the parochial church council.

F 15   Of churches not to be profaned

1   The churchwardens and their assistants shall not suffer the
church or chapel to be profaned by any meeting therein for

temporal objects inconsistent with the sanctity of the place, nor the bells to be rung at any time contrary to the direction of the minister.

2   They shall not suffer any person so to behave in the church, church porch, or churchyard during the time of divine service as to create disturbance. They shall also take care that nothing be done therein contrary to the law of the Church or of the Realm.

3   If any person be guilty of riotous, violent, or indecent behaviour in any church, chapel, or churchyard, whether in any time of divine service or not, or of disturbing, vexing, troubling, or misusing any minister officiating therein, the said churchwardens or their assistants shall take care to restrain the offender and if necessary proceed against him according to law.

F 16   Of plays, concerts, and exhibitions of films and pictures in churches

1   When any church or chapel is to be used for a play, concert, or exhibition of films or pictures, the minister shall take care that the words, music, and pictures are such as befit the House of God, are consonant with sound doctrine, and make for the edifying of the people.

2   The minister shall obey any general directions relating to such use of a church or chapel issued from time to time by the bishop or other the Ordinary.

3   No play, concert, or exhibition of films or pictures shall be held in any church or chapel except the minister have first consulted the local or other authorities concerned with the precautions against fire and other dangers required by the law to be taken in the case of performances of plays, concerts, or exhibitions of cinematograph films, and the said authorities have signified that the proposed arrangements are a sufficient compliance with the regulations in force as to precautions against fire or other dangers.

4   If any doubt arises as to the manner in which the preceding clauses of this Canon are to be observed, the minister shall refer the matter to the bishop or other the Ordinary, and obey his directions therein.

F 17   Of keeping a record of the property of churches

1   Every bishop within his diocese shall procure so far as he is able that a full note and terrier of all lands, goods, and other possessions of the parochial churches and chapels therein be compiled and kept by the minister and churchwardens in accordance with instructions and forms prescribed from time to time by the Convocations.

2   Every archdeacon shall at least once in three years, either in person or by the rural dean, satisfy himself that the directions of the preceding paragraph of this Canon have been carried out in all the parishes within his jurisdiction.

F 18   Of the survey of churches

Every archdeacon shall survey the churches, chancels, and churchyards within his jurisdiction at least once in three years, either in person or by the rural dean, and shall give direction for the amendment of all defects in the fabric, ornaments, and furniture of the same. In particular he shall exercise the powers conferred upon him by the Inspection of Churches Measure, 1954.

Section G

THE ECCLESIASTICAL COURTS

G 1   Of Ecclesiastical Courts and Commissions

The Ecclesiastical Courts which are or may be constituted in accordance with the provisions of the Ecclesiastical Jurisdiction Measure, 1963, are as follows:

1   For each diocese the court of the bishop thereof, called the Consistory Court of the diocese or, in the case of the diocese of Canterbury, the Commissary Court thereof, for the trial of offences against the laws ecclesiastical not involving matter of doctrine, ritual, or ceremonial and also of faculty and other causes as provided in the Ecclesiastical Jurisdiction Measure.

2   For each of the provinces of Canterbury and York

a   a court of the archbishop (to be called in the case of the court of the province of Canterbury the Arches Court of Canterbury, and, in the case of the court for the province of York, the Chancery Court of York) having appellate jurisdiction as provided in the Ecclesiastical Jurisdiction Measure.

b   Commissions appointed by the Upper House of the Convocation of the province for the trial of a bishop for an offence against the laws ecclesiastical, other than an offence involving matter of doctrine, ritual, or ceremonial.

3   For both of the said provinces

a   a court called the Court of Ecclesiastical Causes Reserved for the trial of offences against the laws ecclesiastical involving doctrine, ritual, or ceremonial and all suits of *duplex querela*. The court also has appellate jurisdiction in faculty causes involving doctrine, ritual, or ceremonial.

b   Commissions appointed by the Upper House of the Convocations of both the said provinces for the trial of an archbishop for an offence against the laws ecclesiastical, other than an offence involving matter of doctrine, ritual, or ceremonial.

4   There may be appointed by Her Majesty a Commission of Review, to review any finding of the Court of Ecclesiastical Causes Reserved or of any Commission of the Upper House of the Convocations appointed for the trial of a bishop or an archbishop.

5   Her Majesty in Council has jurisdiction to hear appeals from the Court of Arches or the Chancery Court in faculty causes not involving matter of doctrine, ritual, or ceremonial.

G 2   Of the chancellor or judge of a Consistory Court

1   The judge of the Consistory Court of a diocese is styled the chancellor of the diocese or, in the case of the diocese of Canterbury, the commissary general, and is appointed by the bishop of the diocese.

2   The qualifications of a person appointed to be chancellor of a diocese are that he shall be at least thirty years old and either a barrister at law of at least seven years' standing or a person who has held high judicial office. Before appointing a layman, the bishop must satisfy himself that the person to be appointed is a communicant.

3   The chancellor of a diocese, before he enters on the execution of his office, is required to take and subscribe, either before the bishop of the diocese in the presence of the diocesan registrar, or in open court in the presence of the registrar

a   the Oath of Allegiance, in the same form as in Canon C 13;
b   the following oath:

I, A.B., do swear that I will, to the uttermost of my understanding, deal uprightly and justly in my office, without respect of favour or reward: So help me God.

If he is a layman, he is also required to make and subscribe, in the like circumstances, the Declaration of Assent in the following form:

I, A.B., do solemnly make the following declaration: I assent to the Thirty-nine Articles of Religion, and to the Book of Common Prayer and of the Ordering of Bishops, Priests, and Deacons. I believe the doctrine of the Church of England as therein set forth to be agreeable to the Word of God.

G 3   Of the judges of the Arches Court of Canterbury and the Chancery Court of York

1   The judges of the Arches Court of Canterbury and the Chancery Court of York respectively are five in number.

2   Of the judges of each of the said courts:

a   one, who is a judge of both courts (and, in respect of his jurisdiction in the province of Canterbury, is styled Dean of the Arches and, in respect of his jurisdiction in the province of

York, is styled Auditor) is appointed by the Archbishops of Canterbury and York jointly with the approval of Her Majesty;

b   two are persons in holy orders appointed by the Prolocutor of the Lower House of the Convocation of the relevant province;

c   two are laymen appointed by the Chairman of the House of Laity after consultation with the Lord Chancellor and possessing such judicial experience as the Lord Chancellor thinks appropriate.

3   The qualifications of a person appointed to be Dean of the Arches and Auditor are that he should be either a barrister at law of at least ten years' standing or a person who has held high judicial office, and, before appointing a layman, the archbishops must satisfy themselves that he is a communicant.

4   Before the Chairman of the House of Laity appoints a person to be a judge of either of the said courts, he must satisfy himself that that person is a communicant.

5   The Dean of the Arches and Auditor, before he enters on the execution of his office, is required to take and subscribe

i   before the Archbishop of Canterbury in the presence of the registrar of the province of Canterbury and before the Archbishop of York in the presence of the registrar of the province of York; *or*

ii   in open court in both of these provinces in the presence of the registrar of the province

the oaths specified in paragraph 3 of Canon G 2, and, if he is a layman, to make and subscribe, in like circumstances, the declaration therein specified.

6   A person (other than the Dean of the Arches and Auditor) appointed to hold the office of a judge of either of the said courts is required, before he enters on the execution of his office, to take and subscribe the said oaths either before the archbishop of the relevant province and in the presence of the registrar of that province, or in open court in the presence of that registrar, and, if he is a layman, to make and subscribe, in the like circumstances, the said declaration.

G 4   Of registrars

1   The registrar of a province and of the provincial court is appointed by the archbishop of that province, and the registrar of

a diocese and its consistory court is appointed by the bishop of the diocese.

2   The qualifications of a person appointed to be such a registrar as aforesaid are that he should be a solicitor of the Supreme Court learned in the ecclesiastical laws and the laws of the realm; and the archbishop or bishop appointing him must satisfy himself that the said person is a communicant.

3   A registrar, before he enters on the execution of his office, is required to take and subscribe, in the presence of the archbishop or bishop, as the case may be, the oaths specified in paragraph 3 of Canon G 2, and to make and subscribe, in the like presence, the declaration therein specified.

G 5   Of visitations

1   Every archbishop, bishop, and archdeacon has the right to visit, at times and places limited by law or custom, the province, diocese, or archdeaconry committed to his charge, in a more solemn manner, and in such visitation to perform all such acts as by law and custom are assigned to his charge in that behalf for the edifying and well-governing of Christ's flock, that means may be taken thereby for the supply of such things as are lacking and the correction of such things as are amiss.

2   During the time of such visitation the jurisdiction of all inferior Ordinaries shall be suspended save in places which by law or custom are exempt.

G 6   Of presentments

1   Every archbishop, bishop, and archdeacon, and every other person having ecclesiastical jurisdiction, when they summon their visitation, shall deliver or cause to be delivered to the minister and churchwardens of every parish, or to some of them, such articles of inquiry, as they, or any of them, shall require the minister and churchwardens to ground their presentments upon.

2   With the said articles shall be delivered the form of declaration which must be made immediately before any such presentment, to the intent that the minister and churchwardens having had beforehand sufficient time to consider both what their said declarations shall be, and also the articles upon which they are to ground their presentments, may frame them advisedly and truly according to their consciences.

Proviso to Canon 113 of the Code of 1603

Provided always, That if any man confess his secret and hidden sins to the Minister, for the unburdening of his conscience, and to receive spiritual consolation and ease of mind from him; we do not any way bind the said Minister by this our Constitution, but do straitly charge and admonish him, that he do not at any time reveal and make known to any person whatsoever any crime or offence so committed to his trust and secrecy, (except they be such crimes as by the laws of this realm his own life may be called into question for concealing the same,) under pain of irregularity.

INDEX

INDEX